ISBN 978-0-243-10614-1
PIBN 10786200

HOW TO PRAY.

TRANSLATED FROM THE FRENCH OF

ABBÉ GROU, S.J.,

BY

TERESA FITZGERALD.

EDITED WITH PREFACE

BY

FATHER CLARKE, S.J.

———

SECOND EDITION.

———

London:
THOMAS BAKER, SOHO SQUARE.

PREFACE.

THERE are very few Christians who have not learned by their own experience how difficult it is to pray, or at all events to pray well. Anyone who will teach us how to pray is a friend indeed, to whom we can never be as grateful as we ought. Such a friend we have in Père Grou, S.J., the author of the following pages, which are but a portion of his larger work, "L'Ecole de Jésus Christ." It is a privilege, both for the translator and myself, that we have taken a part in introducing them to English readers, and we do so with a confident belief that they will be a source of comfort and encouragement to many a poor disconsolate soul that has long struggled against aridity and desolation in prayer, and will enable many, whose prayers have hitherto been imperfect and ill-directed, to pray better than they have ever done before.

R. F. CLARKE, S.J.

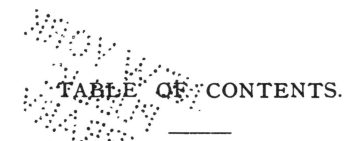

TABLE OF CONTENTS.

———

CHAPTER I.

God alone can Teach us How to Pray.

THE Apostles once said to Jesus Christ: *"Lord, teach us to pray."**

It was the Holy Ghost who inspired this request, and who, then and there, gave them the most perfect idea of prayer, by means of which the creature draws nigh to God, adores Him, gives Him thanks, begs pardon for his offences, and lays before Him his needs. Filling them with a sense of their own nothingness and of the greatness of God, the Holy Ghost convinced them of their inability to perform these supernatural acts unaided, and He drew them interiorly to have recourse to Jesus Christ as the only Master who could teach them how to pray and by His grace help them to do so. It was on this occasion that Jesus taught them the Lord's Prayer. Later on we shall explain it.

There is no single Christian who is not in the same need as the Apostles, and who ought not, with like humility, to say to our Blessed Saviour: " *Lord, teach us to pray.*" Would that

---

* *Luke* xi. 1

we were convinced of our ignorance on this
great subject, and the need we have of such a
Master as Jesus Christ ! Oh, if only we would
make our petition to Him with confidence, and
entreat Him to instruct us Himself, sincerely
wishing to be the disciples of His grace in the
science of conversing with God, how soon should
we become versed in this science, and make
ourselves acquainted with many of its most
secret mysteries. It is not enough to say that
Jesus has taught us through His apostles, and
that we know the prayer they learnt from Him.
The words, indeed, of that prayer we know, but
without His grace we cannot understand their
meaning, and can neither ask nor obtain what
it expresses. We are outwardly taught, as
were the Apostles, when our Blessed Saviour
complied with their request, but that is not
enough. We must, like them, be taught inwardly;
and this teaching they received only when the
Holy Ghost came down upon them at Pentecost.
Then it was that, thanks to their humble request,
they received the sublime gift of prayer which
was bestowed upon them by the Most Holy
Spirit.

What is it that prevents us from receiving this
same gift in that degree in which it shall be the
good pleasure of God to communicate it ? Can
we doubt that Jesus Christ is anxious to grant it

to us ? But do we ourselves desire it ? Do **we
ask** for it ? Do we feel the need of it ? How
many Christians, alas! do not even know what
it is! And how many, too, instead of wishing
for it, dread it, because it would bind them **to**
aim at a perfection which they have abandoned.

We know by heart some set forms of prayer,
others we find in books at our desire; this
satisfies us when we have read them or récited
them from memory; we think not of anything
more being required. How grievously mistaken
are we! With all these forms, however beautiful
may be the sentiments they express, we do not
know how to pray, and during most of the time
we are not praying at all, or rather we are
praying according to our own fancy, not as God
wishes. Where is the Christian who would not
be offended, were he told he did not know how
to pray ? And where is he whose chief prayer
consists in begging God to teach him how to
pray ? Nevertheless it is a fact that nearly all
are very ignorant on this subject, and it is a
fact that no one but God alone can instruct us
by speaking to our heart; finally, it is a fact that
none but spiritually minded persons, animated
by the grace of God can pray according to His
mind, whatever may be their prayer, whether
vocal or mental.

To come now to something more definite, I

affirm that it is necessary that God should teach us everything concerning the nature of prayer, its *objects*, its *qualities*, the *dispositions* it requires, and the *personal application* we must make of it according to our needs. This is to say that in the matter of prayer we are as ignorant of the theory as we are of the practice.

We know in general that prayer is an act of religion, but when there is a question of our own payers we easily lose sight of the truth that it is a supernatural act, which consequently is above our strength, and is one which we can only acquit ourselves worthily by the inspiration and help of grace. Thus St. Paul says : *"Not that we are sufficient to think anything of ourselves, as of ourselves, but our sufficiency is from God."**

Have we habitually this thought in our mind, and in our heart the feeling of our own insufficiency ? Do we acknowledge it when we place ourselves in the presence of God ? Is it with this intimate avowal of our weakness that we begin our prayers ? I do not say we must always expressly invoke God's help, but it should ever be in our heárt, and this disposition should be predominant during the whole course of our prayer.

Now, if we are to expect all from God, all our good thoughts and all our good feelings,

---

* 2 *Cor.* iii. 5.

how is it that some people are so blind and careless that they content themselves with coldly reciting their prayers, without any preparation, as if it sufficed to have merely memory and eyes ? And why are some persons so indiscreet as to strain their heads, get agitated, and work up their imagination as if all depended on their own efforts, and the action of God should neither order nor direct their own ? As prayer is a supernatural act we must earnestly entreat of God that He would bring it about in our heart and then we must peacefully make it under His direction, by our fervour we must draw down divine grace, and then we must correspond to it without interfering with its effects.

If God does not teach us we shall never thoroughly know the nature of prayer, and it is not going too far to say that many people, even though they are otherwise clever and learned, have no knowledge of it.

"*God*," says Jesus Christ, "*is a Spirit, and they that adore him, must adore him in spirit and in truth.*"* Prayer therefore is wholly a spiritual act, directed to Him who is the Spirit of spirits, the Spirit who sees all things and who is, as St. Augustine says, more intimately present to our soul than its deepest depths. If we add to what is of the essence of prayer certain bodily

* *John* iv 24

postures, words, external marks of devotion; all these of themselves mean nothing, and are only pleasing to God inasmuch as they express the sentiments of the soul. It is, properly speaking, the *heart* that prays; it is to the voice of the heart that God lends an attentive ear. Whoever speaks of the heart means that which is most spiritual within us. It is indeed noteworthy that in Holy Scripture prayer is always attributed to the heart; it is moreover the heart that God teaches and it is the heart, when instructed how to pray, that afterwards enlightens the understanding.

If this be the case, and we cannot doubt that it is, why do we pray so much with the lips and so little with the heart? Why do we not draw our prayer from this source, instead of having recourse to our memory and our lips? Why in meditation is there so much mental labour expended in seeking for reflections and so little action of the will moving it to make acts of love? And why, furthermore, do we not simply lay open our heart before God, begging of Him to place therein whatever prayer is most pleasing to Himself? Can we consider any method faulty which is the fruit of humility, of the deep feeling of our own incapacity, of a lively faith and confidence in God, and is a method of prayer that the Holy Ghost Himself suggests, to those souls that apply to Him that they may learn how to pray ?

But my heart says nothing to me, when I am in the presence of God; if I wish to enter into myself I find nothing but a void, dryness, distractions. To fill up my time, to excite feelings of devotion, to withdraw my mind from troublesome thoughts, I must absolutely make use of a book. What ? Your heart says nothing ? Certainly, so long as it is silent, you are not praying; but if it is dumb when left to itself, it is less so when your lips are uttering words. Do you not see that the high-flown sentiments that you borrow from books act only on your imagination ; that they are not your own, or rather only seem to be your own for the moment. You are reading them, and once the book is closed, you are just as dry, just as cold as you were before ? Nevertheless I have prayed, say you, while reading or reciting these formulæ. Your self-love thinks so, and is satisfied; but is God's judgment the same as yours ? Is God equally satisfied ? What does He care for words, He who listens only to the heart ?

You ask me what is this voice of the heart.

How can I tell you ? And how could you understand me ? The voice of the heart is love. Love God and your heart will always be speaking to Him ; it will always be praying to Him.

The germ of love is the germ of prayer; the development and the perfection of love are the development and perfection of prayer. If you do not understand this, you have never yet loved and never prayed. Beg of God to open your heart and light it up with one spark of His love; then will you begin to understand what it is to pray.

But, some may say, does a sinner who prays to God from his heart already love Him? Yes; at least he has a beginning of love, otherwise how could he pray from his heart? And it is this love that dictates his prayer. It may not as yet be strong enough to justify him; but it prepares and leads him on to justification. But what about the just man who is distracted, cold and insensible in his prayer? Does not he love God? If it is through his own fault that he is in this disposition, he may have habitual love, as we are supposing him to be a just man; but at this moment he makes no use of his habit of love; love is dormant; he does not pray, his heart is idle, while his tongue is in motion.

Holy souls, who are undergoing the painful trial of dryness and aridity, and whose love is so much the purer, as it is less sensible, must not be alarmed; what has just been said does not apply to them.

If it is the heart that prays, evidently it can sometimes and even habitually pray alone, without

words, either expressed or mental. This is just
what few people understand and many deny
altogether. They must have express and formal
acts, at least interior, that are distinctly perceived,
and of which the soul is conscious; without
such acts they recognise no prayer. They are
however mistaken and God has not yet taught
them how the heart prays. It prays in the same
way as the mind thinks. Now thought is formed
in the mind before it can be clothed in words.
The proof of this is that words are often sought,
and one after the other are rejected till the words
are met with that best express our thought. We
want words to make ourselves understood by
others; but they are useless for ourselves, and
if we were pure spirits we should need no
language either for the formation or for the
communication of our thoughts. So it is with
the feelings of the heart; it conceives them, it
adopts them, and puts them in practice, without
there being any necessity of words, unless it
would communicate them to our fellow men, or
bear testimony of them to ourselves.

God reads the secret of hearts, He penetrates
into the very depths of our most intimate feelings,
of those even that are not reflected upon, or
perceived even by the soul. And if these feelings
are religious and supernatural, how can He do
otherwise than see them, since He Himself

inspired them by His grace and helps our will
to consent to them ? Hence it is not necessary
that we should have recourse to formal acts,
even when purely and simply interior, to make
ourselves heard by God ; and if we do make use
of these in our prayers, it is less for Him than
ourselves, that we may keep up our attention in
His presence. Our weakness often requires the
help of these acts ; but they are not the essence
of prayer, and God, when it so pleases Him,
raises the soul occasionally above this need.

Suppose then, a soul so united to God, that
to be attentive to prayer it needs no longer
explicit acts in these moments of silence and of
peace when it heeds not what is passing within
it. It prays, and excellently too, with a simple,
straightforward prayer that God hears perfectly,
although the soul cannot perceive it, being as
it were transported out of self by the action of
divine grace. The heart is full of thoughts of
God, which it is unable to express clearly, and
which are so spiritual that they escape its knowledge, but they are not unknown to God. This
prayer so empty of all images, and seemingly
inactive, is yet so active that it is, as far as
it can be so in this life, pure adoration in
spirit and in truth ; the adoration that is really
worthy of God where the soul is united to Him
in its very depths, the created intelligence to

the increated intelligence, without the medium
of the imagination or of the reasoning powers,
or anything beyond a very simple attention of
the understanding, and an equally simple application of the will. This is what is called prayer
of silence, the prayer of quiet, of simple contemplation, of pure faith, to which God raises
by degrees those who have given themselves
entirely to Him, and whom He governs by His
grace in a most especial manner.

The souls favoured with this excellent gift,
who read this, will easily understand it, and
they will recognize in this the prayer that keeps
them as it were annihilated before God, and lost
in Him. Others will understand nothing of it,
and (using the gospel phrase) it will be a hidden
word to them. Let these begin by respecting
what they cannot understand, let them desire to
experience the same in order that they may
understand it, let it be the object of their prayers,
and let them live in such a way as to deserve
that God should listen to their prayer.

If there be one favour more than another,
which God desires to communicate to us, it is
this ; but where are the Christians who dispose
themselves to receive it by detachment and purity
of heart ? Where are they who having received
the first-fruits of it know how to cultivate them
by unreserved correspondence to grace ?

Those who cannot conceive how the heart can pray alone and without any distinct acts, are equally unable to understand how a simple general prayer virtually contains all particular prayers. I except vocal prayers of obligation, and were I not to specify this exception it would be sufficiently understood of itself. In this these people treat with God as they do with men, thinking they are not understood unless they go into detailed explanations of the things they require. They carefully get ready their intention, they have express forms for each and every act, they name separately each person they wish to pray for, and if the least detail escapes their memory they do not think that God can supply it. Souls of little faith, and who know not God, your intentions are present to Him before you open your mouth! He sees them as soon as they are formed in your heart; what need have you to torment yourselves in explaining them to Him? You desire all spiritual blessings as much for yourselves as for those in whom you take an interest. Is He ignorant of this, since He Himself inspires you with these desires? Do not then have any anxiety concerning this matter. If you feel drawn to this simple and general prayer of which I speak, do not give it up under the pretext that it aims at no particular object, that you come from it without having asked for anything. Here again you are deceiving yourself; you have asked for everything you need for yourself and for those belonging to you, far better than if you had specified each want of which the multiplicity would only have wearied you and hindered the action of God which is working to keep you in a holy calm in His presence.

After this short explanation you will admit that, till now, you have not known the nature of prayer. If you begin to conceive a different idea of it, thank God who is inwardly enlightening you, and who inspires me to say what I am now writing for your instruction.

O my blessed Saviour! How greatly I needed instructions on prayer! How could I have been ignorant of the fact that it is an entirely supernatural act, and that Thy grace alone could produce it in hearts that are well disposed. I thought that it was sufficient to repeat the prayers taught me in my childhood, adding thereto certain forms found in books, and that in repeating or reading these I was fulfilling, in every particular, the first of all my duties. How greatly was I mistaken! I never dreamt that words are the mere raw material of prayer, that the heart alone prays, and that to converse with Thee any other language but that of the heart is useless. O language of the heart, so expressive and powerful with God, language of the blessed spirits, and which the saints endeavour to learn on earth, I have never known how to make use of you in speaking to God.

O my Divine Master! teach me this silent language that says so much. Teach me to keep myself in interior and exterior silence in Thy presence; to adore Thee from the very depths of my being, to expect all from Thee without asking for anything but the fulfilment of Thy will. Teach me to let Thee act upon my soul and in it produce the simple and general prayer which puts nothing into words, and says everything, which specifies nothing and includes everything. If Thou grantest me this grace how faithfully shall I consecrate to Thee a fixed time each day for prayer! With what joy shall I fulfil this duty, and what care shall I not always take to preserve so precious a gift! But O Lord I know not what I am saying. I speak as if I were capable of making promises, or keeping them, if made, by my own strength, and as if my promises could cause Thee to do me any good. I look at Thy bounty alone; grant me this favour for the glory of Thy name, and add the grace of making good use of it and of meriting its increase. *Amen.*

CHAPTER II.

God alone can Teach us How to Pray.

THE teaching of our Saviour is no less necessary to the greater number of Christians as to the *motive* or *end* of prayer. I mean above all the interior teaching of grace, which not only enlightens the understanding but acts upon the will to make it resolve to carry out in practice what it knows in theory.

Prayer, like sacrifice has four ends: *Adoration, Thanksgiving, Propitiation* or obtaining forgiveness of sins, and *Impetration* or procuring of goods, spiritual or temporal.

The two first ends refer directly to God, and are for this reason pre-eminently and undoubtedly the most important.

The two last relate to our own interests, which are subordinate to those of God, and which we must have in view only after His.

It follows from this that whenever we come into God's presence with intent to pray, our first intention must be to adore His Supreme Majesty, to annihilate ourselves before Him, and give Him the tribute of glory which is His due; the second to acknowledge His benefits, whether general or particular, natural or supernatural, that we enjoy from His liberality, and to return Him for them most heartfelt thanks ; the third to express our lively sorrow for having offended Him, and to beseech Him to forgive us ; the fourth and last, to lay before Him our wants both of soul and body, to commit to His care our Spiritual and temporal affairs, with the firm conviction that whatever He may ordain will be most advantageous to us. I do not mean that each one of these intentions should always be clearly present to our mind, but they must be present in our hearts and hold the place which belongs to them, so that God's interests must be the chief end of our prayer, and our own interests must come second.

Thus in the old Law, the holocaust was the noblest of all sacrifice ; the victim was entirely consumed to the honour of God, to signify the complete surrender of our being to His service, and neither the priests nor the people could partake of any portion of it. So in the new Law, the sacrifice of Jesus Christ was offered on the Cross, and is every day offered on our Altars primarily for the honour and glory of God, and in acknowledgment of His absolute dominion over His creatures. Jesus Christ had other intentions, but this was the principal and all the others had reference to it.

Now, the order our blessed Saviour observed in His intentions when praying to His Father and when immolating Himself is the rule we must follow in our own prayers, and we are not allowed to deviate from it. This does not prevent the immediate end of our prayers being at times the pardon of our sins, at times also our spiritual needs, and sometimes too, our temporal wants, and this without prejudice to other more noble intentions and to the glory of God which, first and foremost, should be the essential end of all prayer.

But self-love, which has as much and even more influence than anything else over all our prayers, reverses the order established by the very nature of things, by Divine institution, and by the example of Jesus Christ. It will not tolerate that when invoking God and in His service, we should have in mind anything but ourselves, or that we should have any other end in view than our own interests. It only thinks of prayer as a request, a petition made to God to obtain of Him some benefit, and it loses sight of the chief meaning of prayer—namely, homage and the tribute of love and gratitude.

What would a sovereign, a master, think of a subject or of a servant who came into his presence only to solicit some favour? What would a father, a spouse, a friend, (for God deigns to assume the titles of Father and Spouse, with

reference to each one of us,) think of a child, a
spouse, a friend, who were to do nothing save
importune them with selfish demands ? And yet
these are the feelings that self-love suggests, and
the line of conduct it makes us follow in regard
to God. We only pray to Him for our own sake;
the end of our homage and assiduity in prayer
is to get something from Him. If (by way of
supposition) we had nothing to expect from God,
if our wants did not oblige us to have recourse
to Him, we should evidently show Him neither
respect, nor love, nor gratitude.

We are His debtors, it is true, and insolvent
debtors to boot. He wishes that we should ask
for the remission of our debts; we are His poor,
and each day we must beg at His door for the
food of the soul and body; but are we nothing
more, and have we not other duties towards God
Who created us for His glory, Who has redeemed
us, Who has adopted us as His children, and Who
has bestowed on us so many tokens of His love?

" *The son honoureth his Father,*" says Christ by
one of His Prophets," *and the servant his Master.*"*
If I then be your Father, where is My honour ?
If I be a master, where is My fear ? You come
and visit Me in My temple ; you prostrate yourselves before Me; you address Me with long and
fervent prayers; but with what intention ? Is it

---

* *Malachias* i. 6.

to adore Me, to praise Me, to testify your love for Me, or thank Me for My gifts? Are these the pure intentions that draw you to My Altars? Do you come to Me to pay the tribute I exact, to consecrate to Me your whole being, to devote yourself to My service, to immolate yourself to My will? Do you come to hold converse with the best of Fathers, with the Spouse of your soul, the Friend of your heart? I am all this in your regard; and you would please Me much more and be dearer to My heart if motives such as these drew you to Me.

Let us enter awhile into ourselves, and be ashamed when we reflect on the low and mercenary intentions which are the links of our communion with God.

Can we not be numbered among those who, like the Jews, seek in prayer but temporal goods, whose supplications are made alone for the fat of the earth, and ask not for the dew of heaven?

When we are visited by some public calamity, at once the churches are crowded; in time of prosperity they are deserted. Does anything go wrong in our home life? Are we engaged in some troublesome lawsuit? Are we threatened with some great loss? Then we become devout, we have recourse to prayer, we beg the prayers of Priests and persons known to be pious. Are we uneasy about our life, or that of our husband, or of some dear child, we have Masses said and novenas begun, we invoke the Saints. Our needs and circumstances awaken our piety within us, as if we should have recourse to God only in times of sickness and adversity. No sooner have things taken a turn for the better, and danger is passed, our devotion cools, and after a short act of thanksgiving to God (if indeed we think of making one) we fall back into forgetfulness of God, and are wholly occupied in enjoying ourselves. Generally speaking it is not too much to say that the necessities and accidents of life are the motive power of the prayers of the common run of Christians.

Perhaps some one may object : Do you, then, blame us for having recourse to God in our necessities, though they be only temporal ? Far from it, for it is the very intention of God to draw us to Himself by these means, and we can do nothing better than turn to Him on these occasions. What I find fault with is that we only invoke Him in time of need, as if there were no other goods or evils for the Christian than those of the present life. What I blame is that God is forgotten as soon as these needs are supplied, as soon as danger is past, and blessings obtained. Really it is too crass and carnal to reduce piety to such objects and to suchlike occasions.

I place just one degree above these Jewish-minded Christians, those who in prayer have solely their own salvation in view, and who are less occupied with the thought of gaining Heaven than with that of escaping hell.

Here again it is self-love that excites and rules their devotion. Certainly such devotion is not wrong, but it is very imperfect. Such persons know they have sinned, they do not know if God has forgiven their sins, nor even if they have themselves done what God requires of them to obtain forgiveness. Hence arise fears and excessive anxiety; all their reflections tend that way. They aim at nothing else in their devotions except to satisfy or make reparation for their sins; they only see in God the vengeance of His justice; and as this frightens them they seek only to appease it. When they assist at the Holy Sacrifice of the Mass they offer it up in expiation for their sins; if they enrol themselves in some Confraternity, it is to have share in the merits of the associates, and in the Indulgences granted to it by the Sovereign Pontiff; they say even the rosary and certain prayers with no other view than to gain Indulgences; nay they receive Holy Communion, for the same end, choosing with this intention Churches and days; and if they perform good works, if they practice mortification, all is done for one and the same purpose.

No doubt this is all very good, and I have no kind of wish to disapprove of it. A holy and salutary thought urges us to detest and expiate our past sins, and to avoid them for the future. What I do thoroughly disapprove of is that all our intentions should be centred in this, and that we never for a moment lose sight of ourselves, in order to fix our mind on God alone. Penance is certainly necessary, but the principal motives that should prompt it are the goodness of God that we have outraged; the claims of His justice that we have denied and which must be acknowledged by our penance; His sanctity that we have offended, for which we must make reparation; His infinite Majesty against which we have rebelled, and to which we must restore the glory of which we have robbed God, by the most absolute dependence; Jesus Christ whom we have crucified anew, and whose sufferings so far as it depended on us, we have rendered useless; His graces which we have abused, and the abuse of which we should never cease deploring. These are the motives that should chiefly excite our sorrow and our re- pentance, prompt our prayers and urge us to good works. Such reasons are assuredly more efficacious in producing true contrition, appeasing the divine anger, and obtaining the pardon of our sins, than the fear of losing our souls, or the desire of saving them. Be this as it may, so long as you pray for yourself alone, your prayers have not the perfection that God wishes they should have, and that charity alone can give them.

Consequently among imperfect prayers must be ranked those that are limited to asking for spiritual blessings, dwelling only on our own gain, the merits we shall acquire and the high degree of glory and happiness which we hope to attain. Self-love has often a larger share than we imagine in our desires to keep our conscience without stain, to correct our faults, and to make progress in virtue ; however small a portion there is of this kind of self-love in the soul, it is always too great, for there should be no particle of it in real holiness which proposes to itself nothing less than the destruction of self-love.

This kind of prayer would be good and even excellent if you could divest it of all self-concentration, if you would look less to self, and only aspire to be a saint that you may please God, because He wills it, and in the measure and manner He wills it. Then the will of God would be your first intention, and to it all your spiritual interests would converge. At the same time your prayers would be purer and would be more speedily granted, as God could not refuse what is especially asked for His own sake. Moreover, you would have more liberty of spirit, nobler and more generous feelings, more pliability under the working of grace, more interior peace, less eagerness and activity, less self-complacency in virtues already acquired, and a more thorough renunciation of self. For all the imperfections that tarnish the brightness of holiness, the shackles that fetter it, the difficulties that entangle it, the obstacles that retard and hinder its upward flight, only arise from our considering holiness only as applied to ourselves, from the desire we have of it only as a personal good instead of looking to God above all and to His glory, and as St. Paul says : " *working out our salvation because it is the will of God.*"*

Putting aside these different classes of Christians, how few there remain who make use of prayer chiefly for the two ends of which God is the object !

The first end is to thank Him for all His benefits in general, and in particular to praise His love and goodness to mankind ; to acknowledge that every good gift comes from Him, and consequently must return again to its source ; to call to mind the many graces we have received from Him, the flow of which has never been stayed by our opposition and ingratitude ; the many sins He has forgiven us, the many dangerous occasions from which He has preserved us ; and thus to run through the whole course of our life, throughout which we shall find ample matter for blessing

Phil. ii. 12.

and thanksgiving. But tender and grateful hearts, hearts penetrated with the feeling of their own misery and weakness, hearts ever dwelling on the remembrance of God's mercies, have here full occupation and inexhaustible matter for reflection in time of prayer.

The second end of prayer is to consider God in Himself, to adore His supreme Majesty, to contemplate His infinite perfections, to praise Him, to congratulate Him on being alone great, alone holy, alone All Powerful, the external, immutable, independent Being; to rejoice with Him at His glory and His happiness, to love Him purely for Himself, to desire that all creatures should know Him, love Him, and obey Him; to esteem ourselves happy to be able to contribute in the smallest degree to His glory; to offer ourselves and to devote ourselves to the fulfilment of His adorable designs.

How pleasing would such contemplation be in the sight of God, whether it presents distinct ideas to the mind, or exists in the heart only in an obscure, general, and undefined manner—I repeat, how pleasing would be meditation of such a kind, what graces would it not draw down on us, provided it were accompanied by profound humility! Nothing could bring us nearer to the state of the Blessed in Heaven, whose never ending occupation is to repeat: *Holy, Holy, Holy is the God of*

Heaven and earth; to sing without ceasing: *Alleluia, praise the Lord;* and to say *Amen* to every expression of His every Will!

What I say of God must also be understood of Jesus Christ, and of the ineffable wonders that He presents to us in the union of the two natures, the mysteries of His life, and the divine economy of His Church. Herein have we matter of contemplation for an eternity, and all that we shall think of it, and all that we shall say of it in Heaven, will be infinitely below the truth.

I will here remark that almost all those persons who limit themselves to vocal prayer, as a rule refer all their prayers to themselves; the more spiritual-minded Christians who make meditation, mostly apply the subject-matter to the amendment of their life, so that their reflections, their affections, their resolutions, have no other end but the avoiding sin, the correcting their faults and the acquiring virtues. It is interior souls that are the only ones who make God Himself the principal theme of their meditations, they being wholly devoted to His glory, His love, and His adorable Will. This will not seem strange when we reflect that it is God who prays in them, who praises and glorifies Himself through them, and rightly understood, their prayer is the image, more or less perfect, of what He is continually doing in Himself.

The effect of all this should be to teach us how great need we have of being taught by God, and of frequenting the school of His grace, because in our prayers we refer all to ourselves, whereas we ought to refer all to God. Would that once for all we were convinced of a truth, which is no less evident than certain, to wit, that our interests are comprised in His interests; that in loving him we love ourselves; and that He is all the more mindful of us, the more we forget ourselves in order to think exclusively of Him!

Perhaps you say: " But if I do not think of myself, of my spiritual wants, of my salvation, who will think of them for me?" Can you, of yourself, have a thought of these things? Is it not God who puts good thoughts and holy desires into your heart? Does He never put thoughts in your mind that relate expressly to Himself? Why then do you not dwell on them, and why return always to yourself? Is it God, or rather is it not your own self-love that makes you leave Him to think of yourself? The very thoughts and desires which fill your heart, why does He give them to you, if not to draw you little by little to a state of perfection wherein you will be more wrapped up in Him than in yourself?

" *My daughter*," said Jesus Christ one day to St. Catherine of Siena, " *think of Me and I will think of thee*." He would say the same to each

one of us, if we were in the dispositions of this
Saint. And why are we not, or at least why·do
we not labour to acquire her dispositions? How
very much is contained in these few words! What
an admirable rule of perfection! What a source
of peace! What an assured means of providing
for the needs of our soul! Jesus Christ declares
that He will look after them Himself, if we cast
all our care upon Him, in order that we may be
solely occupied with Him.

" Must I then," you will say, " put aside every
other subject of prayer and meditation?" No, but
you must wish to be always more occupied with
the thought of God than of yourself at prayer;
when grace invites do not resist, do not confine
yourself, of your own accord, to the matters of
prayer that concern you, and without anticipating
God's action (which you must never do) place no
invincible obstacle in its way, but on the contrary
be faithful in following it, with the counsel of an
enlightened director.

Is it not strange that we cast aside that prayer
which is most to the glory of God and the sanctification of our own soul? Directors of souls, who
do not follow this kind of prayer, humble yourselves, if you will, for this reason, but do not
condemn it, nor deter those souls which are under
your direction who are called by God to follow it.
You would be more on your guard if you thought

of the wrong you are doing these souls, and of the glory of which you are depriving God. There are abuses, I know,—avoid them ; if you do not think yourselves sufficiently enlightened to protect persons given to prayer against them, advise them to seek other direction.

O my God ! I plainly see I have not hitherto prayed as I ought ; I have not known the great end of prayer. Rarely, perhaps even never, have I come into Thy presence with the sole intention of rendering Thee due homage; it is ever myself, and my needs of all descriptions that I lay at Thy feet. Deeply am I humbled at the imperfection of my prayers, and I beg Thee graciously to pardon me.

O Lord, purify, ennoble, raise my intentions to Thyself, never allow me to keep them fixed on myself. Pray Thyself in me, that my prayer be directed always to Thy glory. Should I in Thy presence have thoughts of anything but Thee ? Is it not right that my nothingness should be lost in Thy immensity, and that the sight of my sins and imperfections should excite me to admire and praise Thy infinite holiness ? Be Thou then master of my heart and mind in the time of prayer ; employ them solely, or at least chiefly in adoring and loving Thee ; and may the sentiments that enrapture Thy saints in heaven be frequently my occupation before Thy Altars. *Amen.*

CHAPTER III.

GOD ALONE CAN TEACH US HOW TO PRAY.

SINCE it is a fact, as St. Paul says in so many words, that it is not really we ourselves who pray, but *the Holy Ghost who prays in us*,* and that our prayer is good only in so much as He dictates it, let us see what are the essential *qualities* of that prayer of which the Holy Spirit is the author, and let us apply them to our own that we may judge whether it be His prayer or our own. Here again is fresh matter for instruction, and fresh and most pressing reasons for us to say: "*Lord, teach us to pray*, not of ourselves, but under the direction of Thy Holy Spirit."

The prayer that this divine Spirit inspires is *attentive*, *humble* and *reverential*, a *loving*, *confiding* and *persevering* prayer. If our prayer has not these qualities, the Holy Ghost does not acknowledge it to be His, and hence it neither deserves to be heard nor can it be granted.

We will say a few words on each of these qualities.

The fact that prayer addressed to God, whether

---

* *Rom.* viii. 26.

to pay homage to Him, or to lay before Him our most important interests, should be *attentive*, so that all our powers be occupied with this sole object, is what every one will agree to, and is not open to difficulty.

Nevertheless, how few people pray, or even make an attempt to pray, attentively! I do not refer to youth; their restless senses and lively imagination form some excuse, for at that age complete recollection is all but impossible. The most that can be expected then is that there should be the intention to be recollected, and from time to time to rouse the attention, and, as often as the senses wander, to gently call them back to prayer. But, that at an age when we have mastery over ourselves, can command our thoughts, we should fix them on any irrelevant matters, and bring to prayer an extreme, and almost continual, dissipation; that we should, not once in a way, but habitually, be distracted; that we should never think seriously upon this negligence; that we should make no effort to keep our mind in subjection; that we should have no scruple on this score: all this is indeed impardonable, and yet it is but too common.

I will not here seek out the causes of this disorder; I will consider the case in itself, and I say it is a most lamentable abuse to pray in this style, and the chief source of other abuses that bring discredit and dishonour on the Christian Church. I affirm that this is to offend God grievously and to a certain extent make ourselves more guilty than if we did not pray at all. I maintain in addition that the levity that betrays itself only too readily in our outward bearing, is a scandal to our neighbour, prevents him from praying and often deters him from coming to the Church, where it is less easy for him to be recollected than in his own house. All this needs no proof, and if faith is not quite extinct in those who have to reproach themselves with this fault, nothing more is needed to awaken the most lively and well-founded alarms of conscience.

You cannot avail yourselves of the excuses which children might make, saying you are not masters of your senses. But, you say, you are not masters of your imagination, you are not free to distract your mind from business matters that occupy you constantly, and that besiege you at the time of prayer. In this manner you think to excuse your interior dissipation. Yet you yourselves condemn the inquisitive looks you cast around you, and the useless words in which you very often indulge.

But let me ask you : do you seriously wish to be attentive at your prayers? Is it your first care to recollect yourself and think what you are going to do? If you do not begin by this, if on entering the Church, or even on your way to it, you do not prepare yourself for so holy an action, your excuses are vain, and you are responsible for your distractions.

You are carried away, you plead, by your imagination ! Yes, when you are in the presence of God ; but everywhere else, you know how to control it, if you think it necessary to do so. If you are soliciting a favour ; if you are speaking of some matter that interests you ; if you are conversing with persons of position, you are completely taken up with what you say or hear. Behave in like manner when conversing with God. I ask for nothing more. Am I too exacting ? Does God deserve less attention than men ? And is what you have to say to Him of less importance ?

The visible object strikes you, and fixes your attention, when you are speaking to men ; you cannot therefore really have faith when you speak to God. If you had but one spark of faith, would it not burn up in His presence, before the holy Tabernacle where Jesus Christ personally dwells, and more especially during the Holy Sacrifice of the Mass ? Do not the celebration of so great a mystery, and the solemn ritual, suffice to make an impression on you, and fix your attention ?

You cannot drive your worldly affairs from your mind. They insist on coming back to it. How

D

is this? The reason is that they interest you more than the business of your eternal salvation. For the mind of man is so fashioned that it is naturally engrossed by what most nearly touches it. If then religion were deeply engraven on your heart, there would be no room for any other thought while you were fulfilling its sacred duties, and the recollection of all worldly affairs would be, as it were, suspended. If such thoughts did come to importune you, you would quickly repel them, and it would displease you, that in spite of yourself such recollections should occupy your mind in moments consecrated to God; a feeling which would be sufficient to exempt you from all blame, because attention is in the heart, and so long as we wish to be attentive we are so.

I say this in passing, for the sake of those good souls who are uneasy and troubled without cause by involuntary distractions, and sometimes by bad thoughts and temptations which assault them while at prayer.

God has His own reasons for allowing these; this is not the place to explain them, but two things should reassure these persons: first, their habitual recollection which rarely gives occasion for distractions; secondly, their sincere desire to have none and their sorrow at finding themselves subject to them.

Another quality of the prayer which the Holy

Ghost forms in us is that it should be *humble* and *reverential.* The very thought of prayer carries with it the notion of respect and humility. It is a creature that prays ; and the prayer is made to its God. What is God to the creature ? What is the creature before God ? This single thought should fill us with the deepest humility. What then when we remember that we are sinners; and that God is infinite holiness, we are guilty and He the God we have offended and who is our Judge ? With what reverential dread should we not draw near to Him ? Is it not rather to be feared that we shall carry this too far, and be too frightened in future of going near to God ?

If you have not this feeling ; if when in the presence of God you do not sink down into the abyss of your own nothingness ; if whilst the heavenly spirits, so pure, and so holy, veil their faces with their wings, at sight of Him, you, a sinner, are not penetrated with a religious awe, then distrust your prayer; it is not the inspiration of grace, but mere custom, human respect, or any other motive save of religious principle. Now in all good faith, how do you pray ? In what posture of body ? With what look, and with what demeanour ? Is there anything whatever in your exterior which testifies the reverence and submission so justly due ? Would you have the same bearing, were you before, I will not say an earthly monarch, but a person who held a higher rank than your own? How well we behave then! How our eyes, our countenance, our whole body speak for us! What deference we show people by our very carriage, especially if we are going to ask a favour, to return thanks, or tender some excuse!

It is quite another thing on certain ceremonious occasions of parade when honours are paid to birth, position, or dignity. This, I know is outward show only, and not unfrequently hollow compliment, but why are these appearances kept up? And why does the world account it a crime to be wanting in these outward marks of homage? Because they pass muster as the expression of our feelings. Now as you do not even keep up these outward signs of deference to God is it not a manifest proof that neither your heart nor your mind is impressed with reverence, and that you consider neither who you are nor who it is to whom you are praying? What is prayer if it be not an act of homage? And how can that be homage to God, which in the opinion of men would be looked upon as an incivility or an insult?

The third quality of prayer is that it must be *loving*.

God wishes to be no less loved than respected, and the Holy Ghost who is the eternal love of the

Father and the Son, inspires no prayer that is not all love, or that does not tend to produce it. Love it is, or at least the desire of love, that should lead the Christian to pray : love should be the final object or the very subject-matter of prayer; and an increase of love should be its fruit. Even when the fear of the judgments of God is the determining motive of the prayer of either the sinner or the just man, still love must always be the end we aim at, and if love does not in some measure enter into our prayer, either as motive or end, it is not inspired by the Holy Ghost.

This comes back to what I have just said·; namely, that it is the heart that prays, and consequently that loves, or aspires to love.

When a sinner asks for the grace of conversion is it not the same thing as asking God the grace to love Him ? If his heart be really touched, will he not experience a certain feeling which is a beginning of love ? There will be warmth, soul, life in his prayer ; if it were cold or indifferent the Holy Ghost would have no part in it. If a just man prays from an impulse to pray, with much greater reason will his prayer be loving, for it is nothing but charity carried out in practice. If his heart were cold and insensible, it would be a sign that grace was not working in him at that moment.

Let the righteous and the sinner judge of the

quality of their prayer by this rule, and so discover how great is the action of the Holy Ghost in them.

However, there is a kind of insensibility which is a trial through which interior souls pass, and which frightens them without reason. They imagine there is no love in their prayers because they no longer experience that sweetness of love which formerly was all their delight. They fear they may have given God some just reason for adandoning them, and straightway they give themselves up to desolation. But their very fears and alarms would reassure them, if they were in a state of reason with calm.

The heart that does not love is not in the least troubled by the absence of this feeling of love ; and the heart that regrets its absence cannot exist without love, though there may be some admixture of self-love and self-seeking. In the case of a soul that has made some progress in virtue, love is no longer in the feeling of the heart, but in the determination of the will to do and suffer everything for God, and the more this love is stripped of self, the stronger it is and the purer it is.

Confidence is the fourth quality of the prayer which is taught us by the Holy Ghost.

When He it is who inspires our prayer, it is evident that He only prompts us to ask what He has resolved on giving us, and the first thing He does is to fill us with a firm confidence that we shall obtain it. It is this very confidence that He rewards. He therefore inspires it as a most essential condition of prayer. Our merit is in corresponding to it, and refusing to allow any fear or any process of reasoning to shake it.

We see in the Gospel that Jesus Christ works all His miracles as the reward of faith: *If thou canst believe, all things are possible to him who believeth. Be it done unto thee according to thy faith. Woman, thy faith hath saved thee.* He hardly wrought any miracle in His own country, and He could not work them because of the unbelief of its inhabitants. The faith that He required was not only the belief in His divine power, but in addition trust and confidence that He would grant what He was asked for. He placed this confidence Himself in the inmost heart of His suppliants; often it pleased Him to try it, and He only yielded when He found this confidence immovable. Then He could not help admiring it: *O woman, great is thy faith! Verily, I have not seen such faith in Israel.*

Pusillanimous and distrustful souls, who are always fearing that God will not give ear to your prayer! either it is your own spirit that prompts your prayers; or if it be the Holy Spirit of God, then you are wanting in that confidence which He inspires; and it is for this very reason that your prayer is without fruit. Listen to what the Apostle

St. James says on this subject : "*If any of you
want wisdom, let him ask of God, who giveth to all
men abundantly . . . . and it shall be given
him. But let him ask in faith, nothing wavering,
for he that wavereth is like a wave of the sea, which
is moved and carried about by the wind. Therefore
let not that man think that he shall receive anything
of the Lord.*"* Take notice of the comparison he
makes use of. If the Spirit of God alone were
breathing upon you, He would incline your mind
steadily in the same direction, that is, on the side
of confidence ; but your own wavering mind
impels you, at one and the same time, in
opposite ways ; hence proceed all your doubts
and all your misgivings.

Finally, the prayer inspired by the Holy Ghost
is *persevering;* it is never disheartened; it receives
apparent refusals, but returns to the charge, until
God yields to her perseverance.

Call to mind the example of the Canaanite
woman. God often makes us wait a long time
for the graces we ask for, and this for reasons
worthy of His wisdom and goodness. He wishes
us to set a higher value on His graces and to be
more careful in preserving them, seeing how much
it has cost us to obtain them. At times, too, He
wishes to give us more than we have asked for,

---

*James i. 5, 6, 7.

and therefore obliges us to redouble our prayers. He wishes also to mortify the inordinate eagerness of our nature, which is hurtful to the purity of grace, and by the delay He puts us back into a state of holy and peaceful indifference. Lastly, He wishes to preserve us from presumption, to which we should be exposed if our prayers were at once granted; vain creatures as we are, it is to be feared we should attribute to our own merits what we obtain purely from God's liberality.

Let us then beware of impatience in our prayer. Pride is so apt to enter largely into its every movement of impatience; the least appearance of a refusal wounds our self-love. It seems to us as if God should forthwith grant our requests; while His merciful delays ought to serve only to impress us with our utter worthlessness. Let us at the same time be on our guard against the discouragement which has its origin in indolence, cowardice and inconstancy.

We must be humble and patient; never doubting but that whatever we ask for the glory of God and the salvation of our soul will be surely granted to us in God's own good time. If we are not heard, we may be sure that what we are praying for will not redound to His glory, nor our own utility; and so we should desist from wishing for it. God has promised to open to him who knocks; but He did not say He would not keep us waiting.

He has fixed the time when He will grant our prayer, and He has likewise pre-determined when He will inspire us with the first thought of addressing ourselves to Him. When we have reason to believe that it is He who prompts us to pray, we must not desist, but rest assured that He will crown our perseverance.

Rarely do we find all these qualities united in the prayers of ordinary Christians. The greater number of even pious souls pray more from routine than otherwise. They have a choice selection of prayers, consulting their own taste rather than the Holy Ghost; they recite them fairly well, or at least they are satisfied with themselves so long as the imagination favours them, and the sentiments contained in the prayers make an impression on them. But no sooner have these forms lost the charm of novelty, and custom deadened their taste, than they repeat them mechanically and without attention or reverence (at least interior reverence), without affection or confidence, and they resolve to substitute others for those which have now become tasteless and vapid to them.

Interior souls alone, who, according to the expression of St. Paul, *are led by the Spirit of God,** have all the required dispositions for prayer, and they seldom have voluntary distractions. One cannot see them immovable, recollected, absorbed

---

* *Rom.* viii. 14.

in God, for whole hours, without being **edified** and envying them with a holy envy. God maintains them in a profound reverence, and the impression that the divine Majesty makes on their soul, shows itself in their exterior. Their prayer has its foundation in love ; and even when their own wants may be the immediate object, the glory of God is always its final aim. Confidence and perseverance are never wanting ; they pray with an assured Faith, expecting all from the goodness of their Heavenly Father, and knowing that if He defers granting their request, it is simply for their greater good. Thus, they never weary, they grow not impatient, they do not murmur, but reproach themselves for the least ill-repressed movement of nature. I have but very imperfectly sketched the qualities of their prayer, which rises to a fresh degree of excellence each succeeding day, in proportion as they make progress in the interior life. Experience alone can teach them ; and these souls are so simple, so detached from themselves, so absorbed in God, that they never allow themselves any reflection on their manner of prayer, because the fact of fixing their eyes upon it would blemish its purity.

Alas! Lord, I have but too much reason to reflect on my own way of prayer, that so I may condemn and reform it. I do not find in my prayers any of the qualities essential to prayer.

Scarcely do I say a single prayer with proper attention; I bring to it a dissipated mind and a cold heart. I show Thee too little respect, either interior or exterior, and still less love. My confidence is weak and wavering, I always have a secret fear that Thou wilt not grant my prayer, I do not do justice to Thy bounty, nor approach Thee as the best of Fathers. Hence comes the want of patience and perseverance. I want to obtain what I ask for, all at once, and without any delay; I give up correcting my faults, practising virtue and imploring Thy help for this end, because I am not all of a sudden as perfect as my self-love would wish me to be. How can I become good if I pray so badly?

O my Saviour! teach me to pray, no longer in my own way nor according to any human methods, but according to the inspiration of the Holy Ghost. May He animate my prayer, and ask in me with the unspeakable groanings mentioned by Thy Apostle!* *Amen.*

---

* *Rom.* viii 26.

CHAPTER IV.

GOD ALONE CAN TEACH US HOW TO PRAY.

WE have now considered the nature, the objects, and the qualities of prayer. The question still remains what *dispositions* are required on our side. The answer to this will not be difficult, because we can easily infer it from what has already been said.

But in order that we may come to something practical, and form an effective resolution to acquire the dispositions that will facilitate in us the prayer of the Holy Ghost, I will begin by laying down two principles.

The first is that our salvation and the whole course of our Christian perfection depends on our praying well. For, in the ordinary course of His providence, God has attached to prayer the graces that lead us on to perfection, and therefore we shall infallibly obtain them if we pray well. And as above all graces that of constant fidelity is the most precious and the one that the Christian who prays well asks for with the greatest earnestness, it will be granted him with the rest. Thus he will receive the graces God has destined to bestow on him; he will make a good use of them; and in this way he will, by praying well, attain the degree of sanctity to which God calls him and to that glory and beatitude which corresponds to it. All this forms a chain to which prayer is the first link. This is a certain fact. If a man does not receive the graces he needs, or if he makes a bad use of them, the reason is that he has become remiss in the practice of prayer: the diminution of strength in the spiritual life always begins here. From elsewhere we may receive some slight wounds or have some little falls, but if we never abandon prayer, if we always apply ourselves to perform this duty well, prayer heals everything. It mends everything, and puts everything right. Prayer is a preservative and a universal remedy.

The second principle is that the prayer of the Christian is always good when the Holy Ghost prays in him; and on the contrary it is always more or less defective in proportion as human element enters into it. I have already said that prayer is a supernatural act; it must therefore be produced by a supernatural cause; and the more freely that cause works in the action, the less it is impeded by the obstacles that man puts in the way, the more excellent also is the prayer.

This supernatural cause is no other than the Holy Ghost, who, when he makes us pray, raises us above the weakness of our nature, and who, in proportion as our will seconds His efforts, brings it to pass that we mingle with it nothing imperfect. If our prayer is all from Him, with a simple co-operation on our part, it is all divine, and although there must nearly always be some slight involuntary imperfection joined to it, that does not prevent the Holy Ghost from being the ultimate source of our prayer, since man with the very best disposition possible must always pray in a more or less perfect way, according to his condition at the time.

The consequence of these two principles is, that it is of the utmost importance that the Holy Ghost should be the Master of our prayer, and we should adopt every means in our power that He may be so. But does this depend on ourselves? Yes, it does; the Holy Ghost wishes to pray in us; that is quite clear, for He wishes our prayers to be good, and without Him there is no good prayer. If He does not effect this either perfectly or with the freedom He desires, the obstacle is from ourselves alone. We must understand this thoroughly. If till now you have not dwelt upon the thought, give it your serious attention from this time forward. It depends on yourself alone that your prayer should proceed from the Holy Ghost, and that in time it should be all from Him, in proportion as you let Him take entire possession of your soul.

You will ask me what you must do to arrive at this? You will tell me that you have the greatest desire not to pray any longer of yourself and that you are sensible of the benefit of being led in your prayer by the Holy Ghost. But you do not know how to set to work. You will tell me that the greater the application of your mind, the more efforts you make, the more of self will there be in your prayer; that if you make no efforts at all, but simply wait for the Holy Ghost to begin, you fall into idleness and expose yourself to illusions. Besides, as far as you can see this prayer of the Holy Ghost that we mean is by *mental prayer;* and mental prayer is a gift of God, which it is not in our power to procure for ourselves, and, according to the opinion of all spiritual men, it would be a very dangerous abuse to wish to enter on this path of mental prayer by ourselves.

My answer of your difficulty is as follows: The prayer of which the Holy Ghost is the author, is not only mental prayer properly so called, but also vocal prayer, meditation, aspirations, active contemplation. I agree with you, that mental prayer is the foundation of these prayers when our souls are actuated by the Holy Ghost as we make them. I do not tell you to throw yourself into mental prayer if you feel no attraction for it; all your efforts would be useless. It is not in your power to arrive at it without an extraordinary grace. So long as you have an attraction for vocal prayer, and facility for meditation and a taste for it, do not leave them, and do not attempt to raise yourself to a more sublime state; but always begin your prayer or meditation with an invocation of the Holy Ghost which comes straight from your heart. Recognize the fact that your lips can utter words, but that it is not in your power to pray unless He gives the first movement to your soul. Recognize also that your considerations and affections are not prayers unless He suggests them; and beseech Him to set your faculties to work. After this pray and meditate calmly and without effort; and always remain united heart and soul with God, resisting all that can distract your attention. This is all you have to do, and all that the Holy Ghost requires of you, in order that your prayer and meditation may be from Him.

Notice yet one important point. If when you are meditating or reciting vocal prayers, you feel yourself strongly impressed with the presence of God, and you enjoy a certain sweet calm, and are inwardly drawn to silence, this is a sign that the Holy Ghost is taking special possession of your soul, and that He is communicating to you, on trial as it were by the way, the gift of mental prayer. Then you must be silent and suspend

E

the exercise of your faculties, remaining calm and passive under the operations of the Holy Ghost. For when He acts in a way that is thus sensibly felt, we must in no way disturb His action, but give ourselves up to it by a very simple inward act of consent. If this action of the Holy Ghost were to last some time, or become more frequent, after having asked the advice of some one experienced in the spiritual life, you would have ground for believing that you were called to real mental prayer and would be obliged to follow the call. In order that we may have the dispositions requisite for receiving the gift of mental prayer, three things are necessary: *humility*, *simplicity* and *docility*.

In the first place constant *humility* in everything relating to prayer is indispensable. We must be always willing to depend on the Holy Ghost; we must not rely on our own efforts to acquire devotion, but expect all from God. We must believe ourselves unworthy of His favours, we must not desire them too eagerly, we must not be envious of the souls to which they are granted, we must remain in our own nothingness, and be content to remain there, as in our proper place, we must not aspire to anything exalted. Better would it be for us to pass our whole life in humility and vocal prayer, than that we should conceive the least esteem of ourselves, or prefer ourselves to others on account of our sublime gift of prayer. The greater number of those souls whom God has raised from the ordinary path never desired this grace, or thought of it, and did not know in what it consisted. But they were humble. Their first feeling was one of astonishment that God should have deigned to cast a look on them ; in calling them to this familiar converse with Himself, God above all proposed to Himself to make them perfect in humility, and if they had not corresponded to His designs they would have fallen lower than they were before.

The second requisite is *simplicity* in our piety. We must not trust to our intellect, nor to the subtlety and depth of our reasoning powers. Solid piety is not in the intellect, but in the affections. We must not make use of so many books, pious practices, or exercises, or systematic methods. We must seek in our own hearts for what we would say to God, and then say it in all simplicity without troubling ourselves about the words we use ; it is absurd to try to be eloquent when speaking to Him ; or to have a predilection for prayers that are rhetorical in preference to those simple and natural.

Simplicity is the true note of all prayer, and nothing pleases God more. He does not wish so much studied preparation in His service ; all is

spoilt when devotion is reduced to a system, and so
much careful arrangement is thought necessary.
After all we must ever go back to the Holy Spirit;
He alone can teach the right way to converse
with God, and when He takes possession of a
soul, the first thing He does is to withdraw her
from all methods taught by men.

There are people who attach great importance
to hearing Mass and communicating according to
certain methods laid down in books of devotion.
It seems to me that to be accustomed to them to
such an extent as not to be able to do without
them, is very prejudicial, because men rely
upon this help, and so do not think of eliciting
anything from their own heart or having recourse
to the Holy Spirit, although true prayer is formed
by the co-operation of our heart with the Holy
Spirit. I should recommend them to try little
by little to pray without books, though for a time
they might feel dry and embarrassed; and to ask
our Lord with confidence for those thoughts and
feelings which He would wish them to have
during the Holy Sacrifice of the Mass. They
should beg of the Holy Ghost to give them the
necessary dispositions for a good confession.
Above all for Holy Communion they should
abandon themselves entirely to our blessed Lord,
and should rest on Him for the due preparation
and thanksgiving. Oh! how much is accomplished

by doing nothing of ourselves, but relying on God to do all in us! I am convinced that we should be all the better for it, as I have more than once experienced myself.

This was the practice of the first Christians who were more at home than we are in matters of devotion, and received the body of our Lord with more fervour and more spiritual profit. Many simple and upright souls may easily be recognised as ripe for mental prayer; they are only waiting for a director who will introduce them to it, and relieve them from the multiplicity of their practices of devotion, which they are afraid to give up of themselves. But to discern these souls the director must himself be imbued with the Spirit of God, and be given to mental prayer.

Lastly we must be *docile* to every impulse of the Holy Ghost. To arrive at this we must study without curiosity, but with attention, what takes place in our heart, and, when we feel that grace is there, we must faithfully correspond to its influence. *"The Spirit breatheth where He will!"** and when He breatheth the soul must not place the least hindrance in the way; her duty is to let herself be led whither He guides her. Constant fidelity to grace is the proximate and the surest disposition to mental prayer.

This goes farther than we imagine. For we

* *John* iii. 8.

must not think that the Holy Ghost will come to us as soon as we begin to pray, if at other times of the day we do not listen to Him, if we repel Him or grieve Him. We do not listen to Him, we cannot even hear Him if we are dissipated ; and whoever is dissipated out of prayer-time will likewise be dissipated at the time of prayer whatever effort he may make to the contrary. Good prayers suppose previous recollection, and recollection is in its turn the fruit of good prayers. We repel and grieve the Holy Spirit when we do not follow His inspirations or warnings, or when we pay no attention to the lights He gives us. He does not fail at first to reproach with this at the time of prayer, but if His reproaches are without effect then He withdraws Himself, and leaves us to pray alone.

That which almost always closes, to a great number of souls, the door of mental prayer, is some simple thing that God asks of them and that they refuse Him. They are undecided for a long time; they promise but do not keep their word ; at last they become obstinate ; then they try to think of other things and make themselves believe they are not guilty, and that it is not their fault that they are not interior souls. How ingenious self-love is in deceiving itself! But yet it cannot still the voice of conscience. Whoever then you may be to whom this is applicable, to whom God speaks in the secret of your heart and says: you would not make such and such a sacrifice, nor overcome this or that fault, nor renounce this or that evil custom, and it is this that has deprived you of so great a good. Acknowledge your fault in all sincerity; there is still time to repair it; satisfy Almighty God and then you will be satisfied with yourself.

I do not think there are many simple, docile and humble souls, who, if they at a certain age fall into the hands of an intelligent director, do not attain to mental prayer. But I am certain that souls of this stamp are the only ones on whom God bestows this precious gift, or at least who have the happiness of preserving it.

Take notice that all holds together in the Christian life, and if you take away one part the edifice crumbles. You wish to belong to the Holy Ghost during the time of prayer, and all other times to belong to yourself? Such a thing is a vain delusion. This divine Spirit will either govern all your actions, or He will cease to direct your prayer. You wish Him to occupy your heart, but only at intervals; to come and go at your pleasure. This cannot be, He will not be dependent on you, but He claims that you should be dependent on Him. If He once begins to pray in you His intention is to pray without interruption, and to keep your heart in a state of permanent union with God; He will bind you down to an habitual recollection, and if you persist in giving up this habit of recollection, He will punish you by withdrawing from you at the time of prayer. He will exact from you a constant fidelity to all His inspirations, and if you turn aside from Him, then after having in vain reproached you, He will end by leaving you at those moments when you are most anxious to retain Him. In this you have no reason to complain of Him. For what does He intend when He deigns to pray in you, and what ought you to intend yourself? Is it only for the sake of spending a few happy moments with God? Certainly not; it is to obtain necessary graces, to sanctify all the actions of the day. How can you sanctify them if you have not God always present to your mind, if He does not act on your heart, if you are not recollected, attentive and docile to His inspirations? If as soon as you come from your prayers you withdraw yourself from His direction, and fall back on your own thoughts, at once you are dissipated, given up to vain and even bad thoughts, a prey to weakness, to the malice of your nature, exposed to the seductions of the world and the snares of the devil.

Examine yourself then in the presence of God and see if you are in this disposition of humility, simplicity, and docility, if you sincerely desire to possess it, and if you are labouring to acquire it.

If such is the case, you have every reason to hope that God will favour you with this gift of mental prayer.

Why is this gift, which God would wish to see generally diffused, so rare ? Simply through our own fault. Instead of desiring it, we fear it ; instead of disposing ourselves for it, we wilfully and often systematically do all we can never to receive it. And why do we fear it? Because, up to a certain point we always wish to belong to ourselves, and not entirely to the Holy Ghost. His direction would lead us too far, would bind us too strictly; we have not positively renounced sanctity, but we wish to be saints according to our own standard, not God's.

I here am laying my finger on the disposition that strongly marks the souls of the generality of those Christians who profess piety. They carefully conceal it from themselves, because it is bad ; but in reality it is this and this alone, that stops the workings of the Holy Ghost and prevents Him from praying in us. We allege any reason rather than this. We are dishonest with ourselves and others. Nothing that God has placed in us, nor any condition, profession, nor employment that is in the order of Providence, is an insuperable obstacle to the reception and to the exercise of the gift of mental prayer. It is suitable to youth as well as to a riper age, to sickness or health ;

whatever leaves us the free use of reason, leaves equally to God the free use of His grace; and it only depends on ourselves to accept it when it is offered to us.

O my divine Saviour! Again I beseech Thee, more earnestly than ever, to *teach me to pray*. Place in me both the remote and proximate dispositions for the prayer of the Holy Ghost. Make me humble, simple, and docile; grant that I may do all in my power to become so. What will my prayer be if the Holy Ghost does not pray with me? And if my prayers are not well said, what will my life be? If it is not a life of sin, still it will be in danger of becoming so, and in any case full of imperfections and subject to heaps of venial sins.

Come, O divine Spirit! come and dwell and act within me. Take entire possession of my understanding and my will; direct their exercise not alone at the time of prayer, but at all times. I can neither glorify God, nor sanctify my soul without Thee. *Amen.*

CHAPTER V.

God alone can Teach us How to Pray.

ST. Paul writing to the Galatians says:
"*Because you are sons*," making the distinction between them and the Jews, who were servants, "*God has sent the Spirit of His Son into your hearts, crying: Abba, Father.*"* Thus, the Christian is a child who prays to His Father. The Holy Trinity takes part with him in making his prayer; the Father and the Son send their Spirit into his heart. Prayer is especially attributed to the Holy Ghost because He is love, and the prayer of a child to his Father must be inspired by love.

The same Apostle writing to the Romans says: "*The Spirit also helpeth our infirmity. For we know not what we should pray for as we ought; but the Spirit Himself asketh for us with unspeakable groanings. And He that searcheth the hearts, knoweth what the Spirit desireth; because He asketh for the Saints according to God.*"† These two passages are the ground work of the doctrine that I have explained on prayer, but in order to

---

* *Gal.* iv. 6.
† *Rom.* viii. 26, 27.

pass on to what remains to be said I will lay stress only on the following words : " *We know not what we should pray for as we ought,*" and likewise these, "*The Spirit asketh for the Saints what is according to God.*" These words have a distinct reference to our wants spiritual as well as temporal, which is the last subject I have to explain, so that this the teaching of our Blessed Lord is most needful to us.

Indeed, as nearly all our prayers can be reduced to petitions, it is extremely necessary that we should ask of God which of them, in His interest and ours, should be granted. He cannot give a favourable ear to what would be hurtful or even useless to His glory and our salvation, and it is not admissible that a Christian should wish his prayers for such things to be granted. Besides the Apostle distinctly says we are ignorant as to what we should ask for, as regards either our temporal or spiritual wants, whether for ourselves or those in whom we take an interest. We know from our catechism that God places His glory in being known, loved and served by all His creatures ; but what in this is the order of His designs, and how He has resolved to advance His glory in given circumstances of time or place or persons, is a secret He has reserved for Himself. We are likewise instructed in a general way as to what will conduce to, or prejudice our salvation, but we are ignorant in reference to this end, what may be the order of Providence, by what means and in what manner His design is to be worked out, and if this or that temporal or spiritual state be favourable to it or otherwise. Nevertheless our prayers generally refer to some particular object, and we are uncertain whether this be for God's or our own interest.

As to the temporal needs, we ask to be delivered from such and such necessity; from this or that sickness or infirmity; to carry out some scheme; that we may be successful in some business; that such a person may live, etc. Have we thought of God's glory? or the good of our soul? Of this we are absolutely ignorant. When we pray we do not give sufficient attention to this. Do we ask ourselves, "Will God be glorified by this?" "Will it conduce to my spiritual good or that of my neighbour?" This thought would often make us hesitate in our prayers and leave all in the hands of God.

We look upon everything in reference to the present; we see nothing beyond, and consequently it often seems to us that our prayers are good as regards their object. But God, who penetrates the future, sees the consequences of our requests and judges differently; for instance, it is but natural a mother should wish her child to live, and so beseech and importune heaven on the occasion of the least accident that threatens him. But God knows that he will lose his soul if he lives, and by taking him at once out of the world He secures the child's eternal salvation. We beg imploringly for health, and we promise ourselves that we shall make good use of it ; but God sees that we should misuse it by offending Him. We pray for the success of some great enterprise, for the favourable decision of a lawsuit that would give us competence, and facilitate the settling of our children, and put it in our power to do good works. But God sees that if we became richer, riches would be to us the means of sin and the occasion of our eternal damnation. Numberless are the examples of this nature, and nothing in any case can guarantee the good or bad result of our prayers, if they were granted. We pray with such anxiety and fervour and assiduity, that it is evident we have some other motive than the glory of God and salvation of our soul, for our prayers are less earnest, less anxious and less fervent when the end of our prayer has but these two objects.

I say nothing of the impropriety and irreverence of imagining that God could favour passions and views purely human, as if His Providence should lend itself to our cupidity and vain projects, whereas our first duty is to consult His Providence and bend our will and desires to it.

We are just as easily mistaken about spiritual

things.   What we think would be to the glory of God and our progress in spirituality is often neither the one nor the other.   I could give a thousand instances of this truth.   For instance you ask God to give you back the confessor He has taken from you.   He took him away for your good; he was an impediment to your spiritual progress, but you never suspected it, because he skilfully flattered your self-love.   God places you under another who will be less accommodating, but with whom you will advance in solid virtue. You beg of Him to grant you certain graces which He has bestowed on others : to give you courage to undertake the like austerities, to raise you to the same degree of prayer.   But these graces that have sanctified others would not be suitable for you and would not be conducive to your perfection.   God has called you to an ordinary life : those extraordinary graces, those mortifications of the flesh, those sublime prayers would tempt you to pride and you would give way to it.   You beg of God to deliver you from certain temptations that torment you, exposing you to the danger of constantly offending Him, and it seems to you that you would serve Him better if you were left at peace on this point. God, however, sees that temptations are necessary to keep you in a state of humility and in a spirit of prayer and confidence in Him, and He answers you interiorly as He did St. Paul: "*My grace is sufficient for thee, for power is made perfect in infirmity.*"* You, who are ministers of God, pray that your talents may redound to His glory; you ask to preach with success, to write for the defence of religion, or for the growth of piety, to labour for the conversion of infidels and heretics; but God has destined you for a hidden life, to instruct the poor and fulfil the duties of a country parish or chaplaincy of a religious community where you will glorify Him according to His Holy will, and though less brilliantly, far more securely for your own salvation.

Into how many mistakes does a misguided piety or a narrow-minded and ignorant zeal lead us! We spend our strength on desires, wishes and petitions, that are not according to God's will, and wherein it would be dangerous for us were we heard. All this comes from our ignorance of God's particular ways with us, the degree of holiness to which He calls us, the operations of His grace, our innate dispositions, and our true spiritual wants. With such ignorance how can our prayers be otherwise than ill-directed, indiscreet, presumptuous, and contrary to the end we have in view? What rule then should we follow?

Are we simply to abandon all our affairs and our spiritual and temporal necessities entirely to

---

* II. *Cor.* xii. 9.

God, and only allow ourselves to make general requests regarding them ?

I think up to a certain point and speaking absolutely it would be better to keep ourselves to generalities. Masters of the spiritual life generally give this advice, and it is for the most part followed by interior souls. Nevertheless as there is no doubt that God often draws souls to pray for some particular object, I think that when we have reason to believe that we are moved thereto by His Spirit, the following are the proper dispositions in which we should be, if we have no moral certainty of God's intentions.

The first thing to be done is sincerely to submit our mind and heart in all our requests to promote the glory of God and our salvation, or that of the person for whom we pray. These are two imperative conditions, from which we must never deviate, whatever be our prayer ; so that it must always be conceived as containing either explicitly or implicitly some such condition as this : *Lord, if my request is for Thy greater glory and for the good of my soul, vouchsafe to grant it me.* Or : *Lord, in this my request I have no other intention but that of submitting myself to Thy divine Will. I only make it on condition of its being pleasing to Thee: if it be not so, take the very thought of it from my mind.*

The second thing to be done is to place one's self in a sort of equilibrium or indifference as to

F

the result of our petition; to be equally content should God grant or deny our request. It ought to be so; for, not knowing His Will (which we can only know by the event), we ought not to incline beforehand more to one side than to the other.

The third thing is not to shew so much anxiety, nor to dispay so much warmth and so much eagerness in prayers of this kind.

We have every reason to doubt of our prayers being inspired by the Holy Spirit if we are not at perfect peace and resigned to whatever it may please God to ordain. We must bear in mind that the soul never loses her peace when she prays in obedience to God's Holy Spirit; for then her prayer, however fervent it may be, never involves disquietude. If a troubled mind accompanies our prayer, or if we are too eager, this is an infallible sign that self has to do with it, or even that it is entirely prompted by self.

While we keep to these three conditions we may safely pray for any want, either spiritual or temporal, and we need not fear displeasing God, for whatever may be the issue, we shall always be acting in accordance with His divine Will. Rarely are these conditions to be found in the prayers of Christians led by their own spirit, and all are so led, more or less, except those few who are really interior souls. Of these the Spirit of God holds possession; He raises them above all personal interests in their prayers, whether they be for themselves or others; it is always God, His glory and His Will that is the end of their prayer. As to the object of their request they have no will but His; they are in a state of holy indifference as to the result, and both at the time of prayer and after, their soul is in perfect repose. Therefore their prayers are always heard, because as the Apostle says, *He who searcheth the heart* only sees in theirs *what the Spirit desireth*, and *He asketh for the saints according to God.*

It follows from the above that to learn to pray well means to learn to sanctify myself; and one can only become a saint by completely renouncing one's own will and following the Spirit of the Holy Ghost.

Now I am resolved: I will no longer follow my own inclinations; I place myself under the empire of Thy grace, may it alone teach me to pray, to live well and die peaceably. *Amen.*

CHAPTER VI.

ON THE MULTIPLICITY OF VOCAL PRAYERS.

"*WHEN you are praying, speak not much, as the heathens. For they think that in their much speaking they may be heard. Be not you therefore like to them, for your Father knoweth what is needful for you before you ask Him.*"*

Thus it is a fault to hold long discourse at prayer, and a very great one too, since our blessed Lord takes so much pains to warn us against it, going so far as to compare these wordy prayers to those made by the heathens. Certainly He could say nothing stronger. We should not have believed that this had been the case, if the Gospel had not so explicitly informed us.

This sentence of our Lord contains instruction of great importance for us if we fully penetrate its meaning.

The Pagans, whose notions of the divinity were as mean as they were erroneous, and who lowered it almost to the condition of humanity, never thought their gods had any previous knowledge of the needs of those who invoked them, and

* *Matth.* vi. 7, 8.

so the latter had to make use ot many words to explain their wants. They imagined too that being subject to the passions and prejudices of mankind, they were not always inclined to do good to their suppliants, so they made use of all their eloquence to soften them and change their dispositions.

Although Christians are far from having similar notions of the true God, whose knowledge is boundless, and whose goodness is infinite, yet they sometimes, either through ignorance or simplicity, behave to Him as if He were merely a man. In their petitions they lay before Him in detail their position, as if He did not know it; they explain with minute precision their intention, fearing evidently to be misunderstood ; they reproach themselves for having forgotten to name a person or a circumstance, as if God, who sees the heart, could not make up for their memory ; they expound their reasons and enlarge on the motives most likely to influence Him, as if His goodness needed to be urged; and they go away well satisfied with themselves, if they have talked much, insisted forcibly and repeated the same thing over and over again. It would seem that, like the Pagans, they were diffident of God, fearing they had not sufficiently made known to Him their needs, and that they could never do enough to make Him propitious to them. This is not faith, nor even reason that directs such prayers; it is the work of the imagination and the senses. Indeed it is chiefly common people, and women in general, who are given to this fault.

Our blessed Saviour did all He could to prevent us from falling into this habit, and to cure His disciples of it; He could urge no more efficacious reason than by telling them that in so doing they were like the Pagans. Therefore He forbids them to make use of many words in their prayers; for God knows what they are going to say before they open their lips; it is not to their long discourses He listens favourably, but to the purity of their intentions.

Not only are we ignorant of those things for which we should ask, but also of the time and manner in which it would be most to our advantage that our prayers should be granted.

All things are regulated by a sovereign wisdom in the counsels of God. The effect which He has ordained that a certain event or grace is to produce in us, depends on a precise time, when He foresees our heart will be in the proper dispositions for it. Before this moment, it would have been too soon; after it it would be too late. What is useful for you to-day would not have been so yesterday, and will not be so to-morrow.

Nevertheless, we not unfrequently fix a time

for God, and we grow discouraged and vexed, if at our appointed time we are not heard.

This is mere pride and blindness! "*Who are you that tempt the Lord?*" might be said to us. "*You have set a time for the mercy of the Lord and you have appointed Him a day according to your pleasure.*"*

Man's impatience is excessive, it can brook no delay; and the holier his requests seem to him the more exacting he is, thinking they ought to be granted at once. For instance, prayers are offered up for the conversion of some one in whom we are interested, or of one whose return to God is of great importance to the Church or State. As what is asked is good in itself, we wish it to take place at once: the imagination is excited, our desires are all aflame, we urge God with vehemence and are irritated with His delays. But God, although He is pleased with our good intentions, remains unmoved. He has His reasons for deferring; we should know this and wait patiently for His time. It is often for our own good, and that He may give us more than we hope for, that He makes us pray longer.

For fifteen years St. Monica prayed fervently and with confidence and perseverance for the conversion of Augustine. She only prayed that he might be baptised and abjure Manicheism.

* *Judith* viii. 11, 13.

But God intended that he should be a holy
bishop, and one of the brightest ornaments of His
Church.   If this holy widow had been admitted
into the secrets of God, she would have seen that
the absurd errors that led astray the bright genius
of her dear son were to conduce to his sanctification, and so also did the intense pain it cost him
to tear himself away from the sensual pleasures
to which he was a slave. Augustine, in searching
after truth and discussing difficult questions, was
all the more distrustful of his own spirit, inasmuch
as his wanderings had been pitiable, and he
asserted more forcibly the power of grace, because
from intimate conviction he knew its all-powerful
action in himself.   I repeat, if St. Monica had
known God's designs on her son, she would have
bowed down before them with greater patience
and submission.   And it cannot be doubted that
the fervent and persevering prayers which God
inspired her to offer contributed immeasurably
to her own sanctification.

Learn from this to pray, so to speak, blindly,
never to fix a time for God, and not to desist from
praying, if you have to wait even as long as St.
Monica. Believe that if your prayer is not heard
at once, it is for some greater good.   And take
care never to allow your imagination to lay out a
plan, as it were, for God to follow. Again I say:
" *Who are you* that presume to subject God to

your fancies ?" Pray for what He inspires you
to pray for, but leave to Him the manner of
bestowing it without troubling yourself.

How many reproaches God has had to bear
from wondering Christians! If only He had not
allowed such a Religious Order to be destroyed,
if He had hurled such a man from his high
station, preserved the life of such a prince, then
things would not have happened so disastrously.
It seems to me I hear Martha and Mary weeping
and saying to our blessed Saviour: "*Lord, if
Thou hadst been here, our brother had not died!*"
They did not know that He had designedly
allowed him to die, that He might raise him
from the dead after four days, by the most
stupendous of His miracles.

Let us then accustom ourselves to pray not
according to our own notions and desires, in
public calamities whether of the Church or of the
State, or of our own private affairs, be they temporal or spiritual.

But as it is the Holy Spirit that must dictate
our prayers (and God lends a favourable ear to
no others), let us beseech this Divine Spirit to
teach us, in praying for the welfare both general
and particular of ourselves and others, to ask only
what He knows to be necessary or useful, both
as regards the thing itself, and also, the time and
mode of obtaining it. This is the only means of

glorifying God and sanctifying ourselves, and making everything succeed beyond our dearest wishes.

Lord! after receiving so many true and instructive lessons, it will indeed be my own fault if I do not henceforth pray well. I now see what I must do in order to pray well. I must become spiritually minded, and give myself up entirely and for ever to the guidance of Thy grace. I must be led to prayer by Thy Spirit only, if my own follows me it will spoil all. But will Thy Spirit be with me at prayer if my whole life and conduct is not directed and influenced by Thy grace?

Does not a child with ever so little reason, who asks his loving father for something, content himself by merely stating his desire, and having once made it known, does he not rely on his father's goodness? Does he think he will obtain nothing unless he importunes him, and teases him without ceasing? He would be blameable if he acted thus, and would deserve to be told that he is wanting in respect for his father.

We Christians and children of God, must behave towards our heavenly Father as we would towards our earthly father and mother. The child scarcely thinks of its needs; its parents anticipate its every want or desire. Is the tenderness or forethought of God less? And is it becoming that having such a Father we should give way to anxiety about our future needs? Would not earthly fathers be offended if they saw this uneasiness in their children? Why should God be less offended?

Because you are not to speak much in praying do not imagine you are to say very short prayers. Nothing is farther from our blessed Lord's intention. He commands us to pray *always*, and *never to cease*. It is vocal prayers He does not wish us to multiply, more especially when they are for the same object; but the prayer of the heart, the true prayer, can never last too long, and God never tires of it.

If we are observant and reason rightly, this advice which our Lord here gives us, is an invitation to the prayer of quiet or silent prayer.

Having simply expressed our wants, in words if we prefer it, He would have us be silent and let the heart speak; it speaks far more eloquently than the lips.

Do not tell me that you only pray with the heart when your lips say the words, and that once you cease, you become idle and distracted. If such were the case, you would not pray from your heart even when you used vocal prayers, and you would only be giving to your words an intellectual attention where feeling took no part. The heart prays, invites, and often forces the lips to be silent, and, if this silence in God's presence is unknown to you, aptly may the words of the prophet be applied to you: " *This people honoureth me with their lips, but their heart is far from me.*"*

The reason our Blessed Lord gives to withdraw us from the multiplicity of words in praying is one that is intended to lead us to silent prayer. He says : " *Your Father knoweth what is needful for you, before you ask Him.*"†   God therefore does not need your words to know what you want.   Still He imposes prayer as a duty on us, and even incessant prayer.   So it is a silent and wholly interior prayer that He expects from us at all times, and He will only listen favourably to vocal prayer according as we are constant in this silent supplication.

How much then are we to be pitied if we do not know what is meant by interior prayer and if we make no use of it !

It does not follow from the reason given by our Blessed Lord, that we are not to speak to God because He knows beforehand what our needs are ; it simply means that we do not instruct Him by speaking, and that it is for another reason that He demands our prayers, whether vocal or mental.

Long vocal prayers are generally the characteristic of those whose devotion is all exterior. Jesus Christ upbraids the Pharisees with this,

* *Isai.* xxix. 13.   † *Matth.* xv. 8.

saying they wished to deceive widows by this apparent piety, so as to extort money from them.* God forbid that I should impute the like intentions to all those who recite long prayers; but with the exception of simple and upright souls who pray thus because they were never taught to pray otherwise, I think there is a great deal of self-love in such prayers, and however so little affectation may be noticeable, there is reason to suspect they have proud and interested ends in view.

Let no one tell me that this kind of prayer is authorised by the example of our divine Lord Himself, who, in the garden of Gethsemani, in that long prayer that He resumed three different times, did but *repeat the self-same words :* " My Father, *if it be possible, let this chalice pass from me. Nevertheless not as I will, but as Thou wilt.*"† We should be very much mistaken, if we thought the evangelist meant to say that the prayer of Jesus Christ on this occasion was all vocal, and that it consisted only in the repetition of the same words. His intention was to make us understand what was uppermost in His prayer. Jesus Christ may have pronounced these words but once aloud, or even not at all; but certainly they were in His mind during the whole time of that cruel agony.

I hear you say: Do you then condemn the

---

* *Matth.* xxiii. 14.   † *Matth.* xxvi. 44.

rosary, which is but a repetition of the same vocal prayers ? No, certainly not ; but take notice that the institution of the rosary took place in a century of profound ignorance, when the greater part of the faithful knew nothing of mental prayer, and but little more than the Pater and Ave, and St. Dominic's intention in having the rosary recited was that the faithful should at the same time meditate on the chief mysteries of religion. So do not think you transgress our blessed Lord's prohibition by multiplying the Pater and Ave to obtain more surely the object of your petitions ; but your intention must be to consecrate a certain time to invoking God and honouring our Lady, in the manner approved by the Church, and this is calculated to re-animate faith and piety in the soul.

The great advantage of vocal prayer, which to be good must come from the heart, is to fix the attention of untrained and ignorant minds, of lively and frivolous imaginations, of persons distracted, or too busy about their worldly affairs, or those subject to temptations. Some of these dispositions are more or less voluntary, and we must try to correct them. In this, vocal prayer is a great help, when it is well made and from the heart. But, except in these cases, it is well to lessen vocal prayer little by little, and apply one's self to mental, whether it be meditation, or prayer properly so called. We cannot give too much scope to the action of the Holy Ghost on the heart, to that action which makes us retire within ourselves and is all peace, recollection, and silence, and will not let itself be distracted by any exterior prayer that divides the attention of the soul.

Let us say a word about children.

Up to a certain age they are incapable of any other than vocal prayer. But, when reason begins to develop in them, would it not be well to teach them that there is another kind of prayer more pleasing to God and more useful to the soul ? Let them be led on very gently ; first accustom them to begin every prayer by an act of interior adoration, and to conclude it by a like act, and at short intervals to pause while reciting their prayers. This is a very advantageous practice, for girls especially, who at an earlier period have tender feelings of piety, and who, if well brought up, might, perhaps, begin at the age of ten years to pray thus, and even to make a few minutes' meditation daily. It would not be difficult to teach the same to boys when they are being instructed for their First Communion, and to induce both boys and girls to keep up the practice for life. The Holy Ghost will act in a very perceptible manner on these innocent hearts, and |will make them taste of a sweetness of which they will never lose the memory. If in the future they leave off mental prayer, this recollection will bring them back to it at some moment of grace and make them take it up again. In any case, if a confessor spoke to them of mental prayer, or they read anything on the subject, it would not be new to them, and they would understand it more easily.

The reason why we are attracted to vocal prayer, and have so little taste for mental prayer, is first of all because we incline too much to the objects of sense; secondly because we want to feel sure that we are praying, and this we do not realise, if our prayer is wholly spiritual; thirdly because we fear distractions, and hope to have fewer by fixing our imagination and senses on a book. It is for this reason that some people pray audibly, not troubling themselves if, by so doing, they are an inconvenience to others. How miserable and thoughtless we are! Of course we must put up with our own defects; but at least we must be willing to be warned of this, and try and correct ourselves.

My intention is by no means to frighten souls, or to make them uneasy about their manner of praying. All I wish is to convince them there is a better and more excellent prayer than that by word of mouth—it is that they should beg of the Holy Ghost to teach them; and then at short intervals remain for a few moments in silence before God. They must not be disheartened, if they do not at once succeed as they would wish; they must guard against the imagination which rises in rebellion against a manner of praying that it does not take kindly to, and lastly they should take to it gradually. I venture to say that by following this course, with discretion, they will be satisfied and pleased to have struggled to overcome their old habits.

At the same time I do not at all mean that vocal prayer should be put entirely aside, still less that it should be slighted, as only fit for inferior minds. It is insufferable pride to think we can do without it; and if we did so, we should infallibly fall into the deceits of a false piety. The most spiritually minded souls, those who are advanced in mental prayer, have their stated vocal prayers for the morning and the evening and in the course of the day, not to mention those that are of obligation, or that are made in common. The Holy Ghost, however strong may be His attraction, rarely puts an obstacle in the way of these prayers. He allows them to be made with perfect freedom; or if He should invite them to put off saying them, it is only for a few moments. I do not therefore think that on any pretext whatever, except in certain very rare and extraordinary cases, we should pass a single day without vocal prayers.

G

But why, it will be asked me, does the Church only use vocal prayers ? The answer is simple. It is because the liturgy of the Church is a public service, and that priests, even when they recite their breviary in private, do so in the name and with the intention of the Church; because the sacrifice of the Mass is offered jointly by the priest and the faithful who assist at it, and who are supposed to unite their prayers with the officiating priest, and to answer *Amen;* and because there is a formula prescribed by the Canons of the Church for the administration of all the Sacraments, and it is not allowable that priests should change any word in that form. Vocal prayer is public prayer ; mental prayer is private and personal.

O my God! I acknowledge that hitherto, either to please myself, or from habit, or from want of courage, I have given myself too much to vocal prayer, neglecting and even rejecting the simple prayer of the heart that is less favourable to self-love, and that detaches us from the visible and makes us more spiritual. I am resolved henceforward to apply and consecrate myself to mental prayer, for a certain time every day. Bless this resolution, and grant that I may be faithful to it. I place myself wholly under the guidance of Thy Spirit, I will have no other Master than Him, and those through whose instrumentality He desires to teach me. In all my petitions I will accustom myself to speak little; simply laying before Thee my wants with the intention of humbling myself and having recourse to Thee as the fountain of all good. Then I will be silent and wait with confidence the effect of my prayers. Give me child-like simplicity, give me faith, give me love; and whether my prayer be vocal or mental it will then be pleasing to Thee and useful to myself. *Amen.*

CHAPTER VII.

ON THE EFFICACY OF PRAYER.

IF there is one subject on which Christ has been more explicit than another, and spoken with greater force and clearness, it is on the efficacy of prayer. On one occasion He says: "*All things whatsoever you shall ask in prayer, believing, you shall receive;*"* on another: "*Amen, Amen I say to you, if you ask the Father anything in my name, He will give it you;*"† and again: "*Every one that asketh, receiveth; and he that seeketh, findeth; and to him that knocketh it shall be opened.*"‡ And to kindle still more the confidence of His disciples, after saying that a father would not give his child a serpent if he asked him for a fish, nor a stone if he asked for bread, He adds: "*If you being evil, know how to give good gifts to your children: how much more will your Father who is in heaven, give good things to them that ask Him?*"§ I just quote these passages: there are many more no less weighty; but these suffice. We must take note here that the promise is a universal one.

---

* *Matth.* xxi. 22.   ‡ *Matth.* vii. 8.
† *John* xvi. 23.   § *Matth.* vii. 11.

Christ makes no exception, either of persons, or things, or time, or place. He ratifies His promise with an oath, swearing by truth, that is by Himself. Who, after such solemn promise, can doubt of the efficacy of prayer? And does it not seem that we have only to ask and we shall obtain, God having so expressly bound to Himself to refuse nothing?

How then does it happen that so often our prayers are not granted? God's promises are positive; they are infallible, and it would be blasphemy to think that He would not or could not keep them. It is plain therefore, that we have only ourselves to blame for every failure.

In a word, it is we who fail to fulfil the conditions to which God has bound Himself. When He so solemnly declares that He will give what is asked of Him, it is taken for granted that we ask *for what we ought, as we ought,* and also from *motives and ends* of a kind to cause Him to listen favourably to us. Otherwise the prayer although made by a Christian, is not a Christian prayer, and God is not bound to grant it, in fact He could not. So that, when we are about to offer a petition, the first thing to do is to examine well if it ought to be made, if there are good reasons for it, and if we may reasonably presume it would be pleasing to God. It is very evident that in making such an examination we must not consult

human notions, we must take counsel with God
alone, whose views are very different from ours.
In so important an affair it is not for God to
follow our ideas, but we must conform ourselves
to His. How many petitions would be suppressed
if we consulted God on what we should ask for ?
I cannot live if I have not the necessaries of life;
if they are wanting, and I cannot get them by my
labour, I am therefore authorized to ask them of
God, and to expect that His paternal Providence
will send them me by means of alms or otherwise.
It is *not* necessary that I should be rich, that I
should suffer no loss in my property which would
diminish my means for luxury, and deprive me
of certain conveniences that would still leave
me a competence. It is *not* necessary that my
business or my undertakings should prosper
according to my insatiable desires; that I should
rise above the station in which I was born; that
I should obtain for myself or my children some
position which I only look at as a money matter;
that I should attain some honourable post that
flatters my ambition, which I am very likely not
capable of adequately filling; that I should gain
this lawsuit to which I have perhaps but a doubt-
ful right; and so on, in a thousand other cases.

If I make such petitions to God, whether for
myself or for others; I do not ask what I ought.
These are so many Pagan prayers suggested by

avarice or ambition, which God could never promise to grant.

I have difficulties, contradictions, humiliations, afflictions, temptations, crosses of every description; if I beg of God to come to my assistance and to give me the strength to bear them, I ask for what I ought, and on this account I have every reason to hope that God will hear me. But if I pray to be freed from temporal or spiritual troubles because I am loth to suffer; if in my impatience I ask to die, it is very clear that such a prayer is not Christian, that it is contrary to the designs of Providence in my regard, and to the teaching of the Gospel which commands me to take up my cross daily, if I would follow Jesus Christ; I do not therefore ask for what I ought, and I should be strangely mistaken if I thought God had promised to grant such petitions.

But, you will say, it is the faults to which I am daily exposed, it is the fear of yielding that prompts me to ask to be freed from temptation; and must not God hear this prayer? No! He offers you His grace as a sure means to avoid these faults, and overcome the temptations; rely upon this means and do not importune Him to deliver you from what serves to make you humble and mortified. If we are going to present a petition to an earthly master, we consider first of all with the greatest care, if the object is worthy of his attention, if it is of a nature to deserve being granted, and if there are no just reasons for refusing it. Does not the majesty of God, His holiness, and even His goodness require that we should take the same precautions where He is concerned, and not offer petitions inconsidered and frivolous and without discrimination, as if our interests, our whims, and passions were the only guides we were to follow in making requests, and that God should grant them all, however unreasonable they were. We are not unlike the mother of the sons of Zebedee, and we deserve the same answer as our Lord gave her: "*You know not what you ask.*"* You would have desisted from your suit if you had reflected ever so little, and you would have understood that such things are not to be asked of God.

Not only do we ask for what we ought not, but we do not ask as we ought, and the one generally follows the other. That we may ask as we ought, it is necessary that the Holy Ghost ask for us with ineffable groanings. And who are the Christians whom the Holy Ghost inspires, whose prayers He suggests and gives them life? Are they numerous? It is not enough to be in the state of grace; grace itself must prompt our prayer, and our action must be a simple co-operation with its movements. But, as to the generality of us, do we know what these interior groanings produced

---

* *Matth.* xx. 22.

in us by the Holy Ghost are? We are habitually
cold, dull, distracted! If at times, our temporal
or spiritual interests make us pray with fervour, is
it not the outcome of a heated imagination, natural
desires, or desires instigated by self-love? The
groanings of the Holy Ghost are as calm as
they are deep; ours are anxious, turbulent, and
do not come from the depths of the heart. The
groanings of the Holy Ghost arise spontaneously,
and we feel they are not under our control; ours
are at our bidding or made with effort. The
groanings of the Holy Ghost are earnest, but
submissive; ours are the expression of our own
will, and we are irritated if they are not granted.
After having expressed our desire, we do not
conclude as Jesus Christ did, saying: "*Nevertheless Thy will be done, and not mine.*" He who
searches the heart knows the nature of our
groanings, and whence they spring, and it is not
the Holy Ghost who is the fountain of them;
He is insensible to them.

Our Lord promises that whatever we ask with
faith will be granted. Faith is wanting in us, and
we carry to prayer a distrustful spirit—fears, and
doubts the offspring of our timid minds, and uncertain foresight. Certainly we do not doubt the
absolute power of God, but, what is no less insulting to Him, we doubt His good will. The
confidence that comes from the Holy Ghost is so

firm that it banishes all hesitation; so patient that it is never beaten back; so courageous that it is strengthened by difficulties; and the less apparent is the chance of success, the more strong it is in hope. Placing our hand on our heart, dare we say that our prayers are animated by this lively faith? Why are we so easily discouraged, if not because our faith is so weak? Why, if God does not speedily attend to us, do we reproach Him with being deaf to our wishes? Why are we dejected, disheartened, in despair, when the storm instead of abating waxes stronger and the peril becomes greater? What kind of faith is that which is not proof against the smallest trial and that is disconcerted with every trifling obstacle? And with such dispositions are we astonished our prayers are not granted? It would be far more astonishing, if, with such weak faith, God listened to them.

Lastly, we do not ask with the intentions and motives likely to move God to listen to us. We conceal from ourselves as much as possible the selfishness of our aims and motives, but it does not escape the infinitely penetrating eye of God, and when He sees prayers thus faulty, it is impossible for Him to accept or to grant them. Any prayer that has not, for its final end, the glory of God and salvation of our soul, He rejects. Where are such pure and disinterested

prayers to be found? Where are the souls that
pray to God simply for His own sake? Can He
refuse anything, when it is shown that His glory is
at stake, and that we have no other intention, save
this, when we pray? What self-abnegation and
what elevated sentiments does not a prayer with
such noble intentions imply! Unfortunately it is
very rare even among the most fervent Christians.

St. Paul says we must do even our most
ordinary actions for the glory of God; how much
more then must we thus perform the most sublime
act, which is prayer! God created all things for
His glory. If we have the same motive in our
prayers, He cannot fail to listen favourably to
them. We have the express word of our Lord
that everything that we shall ask the Father in
His name, He will give us. But as St. Augustine
remarks, what is asked in opposition to the work of
our salvation cannot be asked in the name of the
Author of our salvation. I add that even in the
question of our salvation we must above all
consider the glory of God and His will. When
these two motives are united in our prayers, then
they are truly made in the Name of Jesus Christ.
Never can we invoke this adorable Name in vain.

Do all our petitions refer to our salvation, and
is our desire for salvation principally for the glory
of God? Many souls ask for it only through the
fear of being lost and to escape hell; others for the

sake of being happy and having nothing more to
suffer. I do not condemn these petitions; though
the Holy Ghost may inspire the mainspring of
them, any servile fears and merely selfish motives
are not from Him. In so many earnest prayers
for the correction of our faults, the acquisition of
virtues and for certain special graces, has not self-
love a great deal to do with them? I say nothing
of those petitions that are opposed to our salvation
and would put it in danger. We ought rather to
thank God, than pity ourselves, that they are
not granted. As to others, that are good in
themselves, but imperfect in their motives, we
must not be surprised that often God delays
granting them, till they are made with greater
purity and disinterestedness.

Now if a Christian, in his prayers, desires first
of all the glory of God and his own salvation; is
indifferent to everything else, and is firmly
resolved to accept, without demur, whatever
contributes to the one or to the other; if he
prays by the inspiration of the Holy Ghost and
with unwavering faith; it is quite impossible that
his prayer should not be granted, even were he to
ask a miracle. This is quite evident, because
his prayer has every condition that God requires,
and He having promised cannot fail in His own
word. It is no longer man that prays but
God, who, so to speak, prays Himself and,

wishing to grant something, incites man to ask
for it.

Let us therefore no longer blame God, but let
us blame ourselves for the non-success of our
prayers. "*You ask*," says St. James, "*and
receive not, because you ask amiss.*"* You are so
proud you think you ask properly, and so unjust
that you throw all the blame on God. Let us
begin by learning how to pray; this is what very
few of us know how to do; when we have learnt
this, when we ask *what* we ought, and *as* we
ought, we shall soon have to return thanks for
the granting of our prayers.

But, you will say, one is never sure of com-
plying exactly with every condition a good prayer
requires. That is quite true; tell me where
would be humility, if we felt sure we were praying
well? Where would simplicity be, if we cast a
look back on our prayers, so as to form our
opinion on them? Where is the Christian so rash
as to say to God: You will grant my petition,
because I am praying well. This very uncertainty
about the goodness of our prayer is what forbids
all complaints, and obliges us to blame ourselves
only. In any case, God must be in the right,
and we in the wrong; God is always holy and
blameless; we sinful and guilty. Our pride
would have it otherwise; it tries in every way to

---

* *James* iv. 3.

justify us, even at God's expense; at the expense
of His justice, His goodness, and the infallibility
of His promises, and in this our pride is most
abominable.

O my Saviour! since prayer is my great
and only resource, may I never make it useless
to myself, or even perhaps a source of evil.
Never grant my prayer, if Thy glory and my salvation are not always the principal object and end
of all my petitions. Never hear me, when through
ignorance, self-love or any human motive I ask
anything displeasing to Thee, or hurtful to my
soul. Have pity on my misery and weakness;
in nothing is it seen so much as in my prayers.
Ah! Divine Spirit, when will they be all from
Thee? When will grace alone pray in me;
praying for the entire destruction of self, which
is so full of malice and corruption?

O prayer, thou source of glory to God,
channel of every grace, germ of all virtues, be
thou henceforth the most precious occupation of
my life! How much time have I lost, that I
might have spent so usefully and so delightfully
at prayer! What prayers too have I wasted by
the bad way in which I acquitted myself of them!
It is entirely my own fault that I have derived
so little profit from them; I confess it, I repent
of it, and beseech Thee O my God! to help me
to repair these many and great losses. *Amen.*

CHAPTER VIII.

On Continual Prayer.

THE chapter on continual prayer requires, both on account of the subject as well as the consequences resulting from it, to be treated with care, and read with great attention.

The Gospel says : " *We must always pray, and not faint.*" *

Let us weigh the words : " *We must.*" It is a precept, not a counsel ; a matter of obligation, not a degree of perfection. If we fail in it, we sin more or less grievously.

We must ; it is a universal duty, and concerns all Christians. It does not concern only the priests of God's Church, or persons consecrated to His service by religious vows, but all who profess to believe in the Gospel and follow it as their rule of life, whether they live in the retirement of the cloister or in the busy world. *We must pray always ;* not only must we have a stated time for prayer, and never let a day pass without praying, but make of it a continual exercise, that nothing should put aside nor interrupt.

* *Luke* xviii. 1.

The words that follow *pray always, and not faint,* clearly show us it is thus they are to be understood. First the Gospel ordains that prayer shall be continual, and then forbids its cessation; inculcating thus the precept in two different ways. There is not to be found in the Holy Scripture any other precept expressed in stronger or more explicit terms; yet when taken either of vocal or mental prayer under the name of meditation, it is plainly impracticable. And for this reason those who know of no other kind of prayer believe themselves authorised to restrict this obligation to certain fixed times. No doubt they would be right if God could only be addressed by word of mouth or intense application of the mind.

But the words of the Gospel lead us further, and they ought to have opened our eyes to see the necessity of another kind of prayer, which is of such a nature that every Christian can apply himself to it continually. And what is this prayer? It is the essential, the most absolutely necessary part of prayer, that which alone draws God's attention on us, that which gives value to all the rest; in one word, it is the prayer of the heart. This can be made without any interruption. No other can. So it is evidently this that is of precept, and there is no need of making any restriction of which the words do not seem to admit. It is the prayer of the heart, unknown to the Jews, for which Jesus Christ upbraids them, and that God through His prophet foretold should be the privilege of the New Law: *"In that day,"* says He, *" I will pour out upon the house of David, and upon the inhabitants of Jerusalem the spirit of grace and of prayer,"** a spirit of grace that will urge them to pray without ceasing, and a spirit of prayer that will incessantly draw down on them fresh graces; a double spirit that will keep up a constant communication between our heavenly Father and His children. It is this prayer of the heart to which the Apostle St. Paul alludes when he exhorts the faithful to *" pray without ceasing,"†* and when he assures them that he continually remembered them in his prayers.

But, you will say, how can the prayer of the heart be continual? I ask you, how can it be otherwise? We are agreed that it is the Holy Ghost who dictates this prayer of the heart, whether He already dwells in the heart, or that He is about to do so. Now as soon as the Holy Ghost begins to pray in the heart, His intention is to pray there without ceasing, and it is our fault if He does not; as it all depends on our corresponding to grace, by the entire subjection of our will to His; just as when He wishes to take possession of our heart, our resistance alone prevents Him from doing so, and

---

* *Zach.* xii. 10.   † *Thess.* x. 17.

once admitted, He will remain there always, if
we do not chase Him away. The Holy Ghost
dwelling in the heart would never be idle if He
had full liberty to act. And what would He do
therein, if not the special work of the Spirit of
grace and prayer, and of the Spirit who sanctifies
us. He would keep the heart in a continual state
of adoration, of thanksgiving, of sorrow for past
sins, of supplication for help never to sin again.
This does not mean that the heart would, at every
moment, be making these special acts, for this is
not possible ; but we should be always ready to
make them, when it pleased the Holy Ghost
to draw them forth, and the seed of prayer
would always be in us, ready at any moment to
germinate. This persevering habit of the soul is,
what I call, continual prayer, and it cannot be
denied that this may, and should be the disposition of every Christian heart. It is the
immediate result of charity. Actual prayer is
charity put into practice ; habitual prayer is the
proximate disposition for this.

It is just as easy and quite as natural to the
heart to pray without ceasing, as to love always.
We can always love God, though we are not
always thinking of Him nor always telling Him
we love Him. It suffices that we should be
resolved at all times, not only never to do anything
contrary to this love, but ready to give to God,

on every occasion, proof of this by actions inspired by grace. Is it not thus that a mother loves her children, a wife her husband, a friend his friend? The cherished object never comes to our mind without calling forth a feeling of love; we would like never to lose sight of it, and if the mind is at times drawn off by other objects, the heart never is. Just so is it with prayer. We have the merit to be always praying when we wish so to be, when at every moment we are ready to follow the movements of grace. It would be quite a mistake to imagine that the avocations of life are an obstacle to this prayer. On the contrary, they are, or at least may be, an exercise of it, and there is a prayer that is correctly called the prayer of action. Every action done for God, as being His will, and in the way in which God wills, is a prayer, better even than an actual prayer that might be made at this time. It is not even necessary that the action be good and holy in itself; an indifferent act is no less a prayer in virtue of the intention with which we do it. Thus the Apostle virtually enjoins the faithful to pray always when he says: "*All whatsoever you do in word or in work, all things do you in the name of the Lord Jesus Christ, giving thanks to God and the Father by Him.*"* And again: "*Whether you eat or drink, or whatsoever else you do, do all to the*

---

* *Coloss.* iii. 17.

glory of God."* If an animal or physical action, such as eating or drinking does not interrupt prayer, much less would labour, whether of the body or of the mind, or details of housekeeping, domestic duties, or the occupations of one's state of life. In all this, nothing of itself distracts the heart from union with God; nothing stops the action of the Holy Ghost and the soul's co-operation with it. This is saying little, for every action helps to unite us more closely to God; and to entertain the secret intercourse of the soul with the Holy Ghost. We are always praying, if we are doing our duty, and are doing it to please God.

I rank among the actions that take the place of prayer: visits of politeness and convenience, friendly conversations, relaxations of the body and mind, provided they are seemly and within the limits of Christian morality. None of these things are incompatible with unceasing prayer; and with the exception of what is bad, unbecoming or useless, there is nothing that the Holy Ghost may not claim, and sanctify, and that is not under the dominion of prayer. The *agapæ*, or love-feasts of the first Christians, instituted by the Apostles, were they not holy and seasoned with spiritual joy? Did they weaken in them the spirit of grace and prayer? or rather did they not

---

* *Corinth.* ix. 31.

promote fraternal charity? Why should it not be the same with our meals and recreations, if we resembled the primitive Christians? What I find so admirable in our religion, is that it teaches us to honour God in everything, to pray to Him at all times, and to practise virtue on every occasion, and that there is nothing indifferent or useless in the Christian life.

As there is a prayer of action, so is there also a prayer of suffering, and this is the most excellent and pleasing to God. It is a very common thing for us to complain of not being able to pray because we are ill, we are suffering acute pain, or we are in a state of weakness or languor. Did not our Blessed Lord pray on the cross, and the martyrs on the scaffold? Actual prayer at such a time is impossible, unless it be at intervals, and by short aspirations; neither is it expected. But suffer for God; suffer with submission and patience; suffer in union with Jesus Christ, and you will be praying exceedingly well.

Thus it is that a truly Christian heart can and ought to pray unceasingly, partly by consecrating a fixed time for prayer, partly by acting, and partly also by suffering. And if we take notice we shall find that continual prayer is but the outcome of all the precepts of Christian morality. It is indispensable for the perfect observance of these precepts, it makes it easy, and without prayer their practice would be impossible. Thus is everything held together, the connecting link unbroken, and the one leads to the other.

There is also nothing which makes us better feel the necessity of being interior, that is as St. Paul explains it, of being moved by the Spirit of God *(Phil.* iii. 20), than the obligation of continual prayer. For we cannot fulfil this obligation if we are not in a state of grace, or if we willingly entertain thoughts contrary or irrelevant to those which God wishes should at all times occupy us, if we give ourselves up to affections, which at least divide the heart, and deprive God of a part of it. As soon as we become interior men, then the Holy Ghost takes possession of the soul and reigns there as He pleases. His first inspiration is an attraction to continual prayer; He makes the soul find in this practice a most entrancing pleasure, that fills her with a loathing for the things of earth and draws her from them, so that her *conversation is* henceforth *in heaven.*

All this may seem a vain imagination and exaggerated piety to ordinary Christians, who, through their own faults, have never tasted this heavenly gift, nor felt any attraction for what is interior. " It is quite enough," say they, " to pray at stated times; beyond that, it is quite admissible that we give free play to our minds, provided we do not entertain bad thoughts.

There are also many innocent inclinations and tastes that we may indulge without scruple. What tedium, what slavery to regulate one's life always according to the interior action of grace! However it may be explained, this continual prayer is an intolerable bondage." Thus speak half-hearted Christians who find it wearisome to be reminded of God, and to whom prayer is a heavy obligation. They interpret the Gospel according to their own dispositions instead of reforming their dispositions and modelling them on the clear and express words of the Gospel.

They like to deceive themselves, and they speak evil of what is unknown to them, so as to give themselves the right to live in a careless way and give some freedom to nature. But these lax sentiments will never prevail against the doctrine of Jesus Christ; they will always find therein their own condemnation, as well as in the maxims and examples of the Saints. Besides, it is not true that the practice of continual prayer is laborious to the degree they would make out. If we believed them, it deprives man of all liberty or freedom of mind to attend to his business; it does not allow him to give his mind to the intercourse of life; in conversation he is heavy, always inattentive, absorbed in the thought of heavenly things; alone or in society he always feels obliged to keep serious and to forbid himself every kind of amusement. Human weakness could not endure such an exalted state. In any case to be able to lead such a life one would have to live an anchorite's life.

All this is pure exaggeration. I admit that continual prayer is a restraint on the senses, on the imagination of the sensual man ; and there is not a single point in the moral precepts of the Gospel that does not impose a like restraint on nature. But far from impeding man in the discharge of his duties, it helps him ; far from fettering his talents, it teaches him to make that use of them for which God endowed him with them ; he becomes more assiduous in his business ; he bears more lightly its burden ; and he succeeds better in it. If it deprives him of a false liberty, to which he pays a sort of worship, and of which he makes an ill-use to his own ruin, it brings him into the true liberty of the children of God. It does not forbid him to mix in society, according to the exigency or claims of his position in life ; on the contrary it makes him more easy of access, more affable, more obliging. It makes him take his full share in the conversation, authorises him to exert his conversational powers without any affectation, to be interested and animated in speech, it makes him speak and listen to the purpose, and behave in such a manner that he pleases everyone. At the same time it is obvious that he chooses his society, and that when occasion offers, no human respect ever makes him wound charity, or be wanting in his respect for God or his neighbour.

Continual prayer, as I have explained it, being but a certain disposition of the heart, turns habitually towards God; it does not require a strain on the mind, which is always free to apply itself to what God wishes of it, or allows it at every moment; but its application is such that it is not enthralled by it, and at any given moment it passes with equal freedom to another object. We pray without thinking of it, without reflecting, without anyone being aware of it, or suffering from it. In short, wherever our heart turns, there our prayer turns also; sleep only interrupts it; yet still may it be truly said with the Spouse in the Canticles: "*I sleep and my heart watcheth.*"* I do not see how a prayer like this can have any tedium for oneself or for others. On the contrary it is most delightful to him who makes it, and it can never inconvenience our neighbour who will gain great profit by frequenting the society of those who devote themselves to it. Besides, whether it be tedious or not, it is a precept, and every Christian must try to practise it.

How are we to do this? We must love God with our whole heart, with our whole mind, refer all our actions to Him, and have no other intention

---

* *Cant.* v. 2.

or desire but to please Him.   We must wish to
be entirely dependent on grace, and must contract
the easy habit of listening to that gentle interior
voice and of being docile to its warnings, and
reproving ourselves for the slightest infidelity.
We must also be firmly resolved to renounce our
own will, wage war against our self-love, keep a
watch over our natural inclinations, and refuse
them whatever they crave if it prejudice what we
owe to God.   That is, we must be Christians
according to the maxims of the Gospel, seriously
and efficaciously ; we must go once for all to the
school of Christ and become the disciples of the
Holy Ghost.   When you have taken this resolution, and the necessary steps to put it into execu-
tion, you will pray, or it will not be long before
you will pray, continually, because the Holy
Ghost will at once take possession of you, and
you will make rapid strides in union with God.
If you have not yet taken this resolution, but
have only the desire to do so, nourish and cultivate this desire by frequent aspirations, by pious
readings, and salutary reflections.   *"Ask, and you
shall receive ; seek, and you shall find ; knock, and
it shall be opened to you."*   It is unheard of that
anyone who desired to pray continually ; who
with fervour solicited this grace ; and who in
order to obtain it did all that God inspired him
to do—it is, I say, unheard of that such a one did

not attain to this happy state. It would indeed
be a contradiction in terms. From whom does
this desire come ? Certainly from God Himself.
Does He give it without a purpose ? That cannot be. He places then this desire for prayer
within you in order to bestow that gift on you ;
He will infallibly give it you if you ask for it as
you ought ; and He invites you and presses you
and helps you to use the following language :—I
have never known what continual prayer is, and
I have been far from knowing it. But, O my
God, what I have just been reading gives me at
the same time the idea and the desire of it. I
see it is a precept on which all others depend,
and without which I cannot fulfil them, since it
is the only means to carry them out. There is
no middle course: either I must renounce the
practice of Evangelical perfection, or adopt that
of continual prayer. Can I for a moment waver?
And even were Thy glory not at stake, should I
not risk my own salvation in renouncing the
effort to be a perfect Christian ?

O Holy Spirit ! I give my heart to Thee without reserve and for ever. Enkindle therein a fire
of love, whence shall ascend, like incense, a
prayer rising incessantly towards heaven, which
will draw down without ceasing all the graces I
need. If Thy heart, O my God ! is always
occupied with me, is it not just that mine should

be entirely devoted to Thee ?   O perfect beauty !
O infinite goodness !   Canst Thou be an object
less interesting to me than I am to Thee !   Thy
delight is to be with the children of men and to
converse with them, and should not mine be to
hold communion with Thee !   Unceasing adoration, uninterrupted love are the portion of the
blessed ; why should I not make this my lot on
earth, and thus have a foretaste of the happiness
of heaven ?   Shall I always be my own enemy—
always opposed to my true happiness ?   No, my
God !   I will begin to pray without interruption
in time, that I may continue to do so in eternity.
Amen.

CHAPTER IX.

OF PRAYER IN COMMON.

"*WHERE there are two or three gathered together in My name, there am I in the midst of them.*"[*]

This passage refers primarily to the Councils of the Church, where its chief Pastors assemble in the name of our Lord Jesus Christ to decide on doctrine, and lay down rules respecting morals. It applies also to the faithful congregated in the Churches to honour God by public worship, and also to pious associations that they form among themselves, with the approbation of the Church, for particular purposes. And finally it applies most naturally to family prayers, that are said night and morning in Christian homes. It is on this last point that I shall now dwell. At first sight this may seem a trifling matter, but on consideration its importance will be seen. And first, Jesus Christ declares that He will be in the midst of those who are united in prayer, were they but two or three persons ; we are to understand by this a special presence by which He communicates a particular assistance and unites with us in intercession to His Father, supporting

---

[*] *Matth.* xviii. 20.

our requests by all the weight of His authority. Moreover He promises, on the same occasion, that all that we ask for will be granted us. *" If two of you shall consent upon earth, concerning anything whatsoever they shall ask, it shall be done to them by My Father who is in Heaven."**

In virtue then of this concert and agreement in prayer, what would perhaps be refused to isolated prayer and the personal merits of each individual, is granted to unanimous prayer and the merits of the many. Each prayer taken separately is weak, but in union with others has a strength which God cannot resist. Besides, it is evident that prayer made in common, has a merit peculiar to itself, which private prayer cannot have : the merit of charity, of that virtue so powerful on the heart of God, and that He so ardently desires to establish among men. It is to enkindle and maintain charity among the faithful that public prayer has this privilege conferred upon it.

The first Christians were not ignorant of this, and besides public assemblies were all united in prayer: those who lived together prayed together, husbands and wives, parents and children, masters and slaves. This practice was in force for many centuries. But since then fervour has relaxed. Some people acquit themselves of family prayers as a daily duty, and others neglect them ; some

* *Matth.* xviii. 19.

wish to say longer prayers and some shorter; and a devotion that seems to me rather a mistaken one has introduced a quantity of prescribed prayers, and the result is that people, even the most pious, have adopted the plan of praying alone; there is no longer a family meeting for this all-important object, and each one is left to do as he pleases. Nevertheless, it is one of the first duties of fathers and mothers, of masters and mistresses, to see that their children and servants begin and end the day by prayer. It is certain that if they are wanting in vigilance on this important point, and if it is not duly observed in their homes, they are answerable to God. They will not be justified by saying their children and servants are of an age when they know what they have to do; that they have taken care to have them well instructed in their duties; that they have not thought it well to trouble them in the matter, and that they fear to make hypocrites of them. God will not be satisfied with these excuses, most often pleaded by those who are not exact with their own daily prayers, and who in order to avoid conforming themselves to the rule will not insist on it with those dependent on them. The only means of assuring oneself that this duty is fulfilled, is to establish family prayers, to make it the first step towards good order in the house, to preside at it, and exact that everyone in the household be present.

But how will fathers of families and masters be able to put the practice in force, if they themselves have given up the custom ; if they are not sensible of its importance, and if they are but slightly concerned whether God be honoured and served in their houses ? The evil comes from themselves, and they will suffer for it. They do not seem to know that their own authority comes from God; that if He is not respected and obeyed, neither will they be ; that vice and disorder will not be long in coming among them and taking possession of a place where piety does not reign. They themselves will be the first victims who suffer from it. Every day they complain that their children shew no submission or respect to their advice ; that they answer them rudely and discredit them by their conduct ; that their servants are idle and unmindful of their duties, have little attachment for their masters, and are not at all too faithful. In this they are not mistaken ; but do they go back to the source of all this evil ? Do they consider that the root of this disorder is the want of religion, and that they themselves are the cause of it, through their example, their conversation, and by their extreme indifference about all that relates to the worship of God ? Let them follow my advice, and their complaints will soon cease.

Even though there was every reason to believe

that each person said his prayers privately, it would always be to the public edification, which we owe one another in the bosom of the family, if prayer in common is conducted. Prayer is always better said conjointly. We place ourselves in a more becoming posture; we mutually respect one another; we do not allow ourselves the carelessness that we are inclined to take in private. Generally more attention is paid; the piety of some animates the others; and if the head of the family says the prayers himself, his recollected demeanour, the devout and serious tone of his voice make an impression on the household. If you leave children and servants to themselves they often do not pray at all, or they say a short and superficial prayer. Youth needs to be encouraged by authority and by example; and we easily yield to the temptation of failing in our religious duties, when we have neither witnesses nor a watchful eye over us. In the morning, sloth keeps us in bed; a servant only rises when household duties compel him; and between the two there is often little time for prayer. At night we are overcome with sleep, and as soon as we retire, we lie down without a thought of prayer. No habit is so easily contracted as this, and once formed it is very difficult to correct.

The benefits that result from family prayers are very important and very numerous.

Nothing so much contributes to union, to mutual respect between man and wife, to the holy use of marriage, to mutual support and kindness and confidence. We may say what we please, but men only esteem and love one another sincerely, open their mind and trust each other, as far as they themselves possess, and also recognise in others, a deep religious feeling. And what safer and surer guarantee of religious feelings is there than agreement and unanimity in the service of God !

It keeps up in the father and mother the ideal of the sanctity of their state, and the greatness of their obligations in the education of their children. It makes them faithfully discharge this duty, and be careful of its least detail. It draws down on them the graces of which they stand in need. How many they need at every moment to form the mind and heart of their children ! in order that they may not be disheartened by the faults of childhood, and of the painful and assiduous care it requires; that they may not exceed, neither in severity nor indulgence ; that they may so manage their household that familiarity may not prejudice respect, and that the use of their authority may not destroy their children's love ; that they may love all their children equally, or at least not to show any predilection for one more than another, since this is often the source of hatred and jealousy !

Family prayer accustoms children to a certain religious veneration for their parents ; it gives more weight to the advice they receive from them, and disposes their will to a more prompt obedience. Indeed, nothing can conduce more to their seeing God in the person of their parents than to have a high opinion of their piety. And where can they get this opinion so much as from seeing them at their prayers? One cannot imagine how much the love that God has placed in the hearts of children for the authors of their birth, grows with the estimate they have of their virtue. Grace raises and perfects the natural feelings, giving them strength, solidity and depth. Just compare the picture of a pious family with that of one that is not so. In the one there is subordination, peace, and union. In the other independence, vexations, discord. Piety constitutes the happiness of the one, and independence the unhappiness of the other. It is not possible that a family where, morning and night, the prayers are said with exactitude and reverence, should not live an exemplary and Christian life in every other respect. God watches over it with particular care, and consequently it must be happy. On the contrary, where this practice is neglected, it is very common for one or more of the household to forget their prayers, and in a house where 'this is the case there is no real Christianity; God does not dwell there, and whatever may appear to be the case, every member is more or less unhappy; the husband and wife, parents and children being a continual subject of annoyance to one another.

Another ancient custom that has fallen into disuse is that of children asking their father's blessing before retiring for the night: a most praiseworthy custom, that goes back to the very first ages of the Church, and even to the time of the patriarchs; a custom that Holy Scripture authorises and treats as of divine origin, and which serves admirably to keep up in children simplicity and respect for their parents. Ah! if it could but revive in our day, if we submitted to it on religious principles so long as we dwell under the paternal roof, what a happy change it would be! It is not without a purpose that God has laid so much weight on the blessing and malediction of parents. Noe blesses Sem and Japheth, and curses Cham. The effect of his words has extended on their posterity, that is to say, on mankind. Jacob by a divine Providence, the secret of which was revealed to Rebecca, receives the blessing that Isaac destined for Esau: the descendants of the latter were less favoured by God than those of his brother, and were subject to them. Joseph brings his two sons to Jacob on his death-bed, and he designedly crosses his arms, places his right hand on Ephraim the younger, and his tribe after that of Judah becomes the most numerous and powerful of all. The blessing which Jacob gave to each of his twelve children were so many prophecies that events verified. Apart from the sacramental grace of these ancient benedictions, it is quite certain that God has always respected the prayers of parents on these occasions, and a child that, with faith, asks his father's blessing draws on himself grace from Almighty God.

Family prayers are again equally beneficial to the master and mistress, and to the servants of a house. Masters would have more real respect from their servants ; they would be more loved and better served. Servants would have more confidence in their masters; they would be treated with more kindness and consideration, and would not have to suffer so much from the haughty and harsh treatment which makes them feel the humiliation of their position. When a master is praying with his servants, it would remind him that before God distinction of rank is nothing— that we are all equal in His sight ; that the only real difference is in the degree of our piety, and that perhaps He esteems him less than the humblest of his servants. This thought coming

twice every day before his mind would influence
his conduct, and make him more gentle and con-
descending.   The servants in like manner would
learn to see God in their master, to respect in
him the authority that emanates from God, and
they would serve him with so much more zeal,
affection, and fidelity as their ideas were holier,
nobler, and more disinterested.

All the family or household being assembled
for prayer, it would be a good opportunity to read
an edifying or instructive book.   Such reading,
though it did not last more than five or ten
minutes each day, would sow in the hearts of
children and servants seed that in good time
would bear fruit.

Experience alone can teach us what blessings
God would shower on a home where He is thus
honoured.   Sooner or later vice would be
banished from it ; virtue would flourish ; perfect
order would reign ; every member would strive to
make life one of mutual goodwill and happiness.

To the practices I have just placed before you
for consideration must be added that of saying
grace before and after meals, a practice ancient,
holy, and for a long time in constant use, though
at the present day abolished in too many families.
All of these practices are, I know, small in
appearance, and, nevertheless, it is on these
small things that the sanctification of each home

depends, and consequently that of towns and of states. The negligence, the omission, the contempt for these practices, have introduced first into families, then into towns and entire kingdoms, godlessness and irreligion.

What can be pleaded as a reason for not adopting these practices in every Christian home? Will it be said that solid piety does not depend on these trifles? Good sense will not allow of any one speaking or thinking in this manner, and facts prove the contrary. Will it be said the world has banished these customs and it would be ridiculous to return to them? Just because the world has banished them a good Christian should cultivate them, and if we are too weak-minded to face ridicule, we are unworthy to bear the name of Christian.

Some perhaps will say : Are we then to subject ourselves to a certain rule, and model our household after the fashion of a monastery, have a fixed hour for these exercises, and consequently one for getting up and going to bed? What inconvenience that would be! But tell me, is it not of the highest importance that order and regularity reign in a house, and that it be settled that twice a day, at least, all should meet for prayer? Is there in this any hardship or constraint? Shall we not once for all agree that of all habits, the most useful in every respect is to have our time well arranged, and above all the beginning and the end of the day, which are, as it were, the two fixed points on which depend all our actions ? If I say that the habit of rising late and retiring late to rest, of turning night into day and *vice versa*, has contributed more than anything else to the weakening, and even to the extinction of piety, I should be saying a great and sad truth. As to the customs of monasteries, from which the world pretends to shrink, let it be known that in primitive times these practices were in full vigour in Christian families, and it is from them they were introduced into the cloister.

" But the order established in my house cannot be altered for the sake of adopting these practices." So much the worse : it is a sign that it is good for nothing and wants reforming. All that is an obstacle to the fulfilment by you, your children, and your household, of these duties of piety should be abolished or changed. There is no alternative. There must be no wavering. " But how can we compel children, already grown up, and servants who are not inclined to these new practices ? They will murmur ; they will secretly make fun of it ; they may refuse to obey me." If you are a truly Christian father or master, these pretended difficulties will not stop you ; you will hardly think of them, and you will set all human respect aside. First make known your wish by an open profession of piety; in a short time when your opinion cannot be doubted, express the desire you have to establish family prayers; explain your reasons; say it is from a conscientious motive, and that you feel you are obliged to do so; then fix on a day for beginning the practice, and let it be one of the great festivals of the Church. I do not think your children would oppose you, much less your servants. You do not know the power of religion on the heart. As to murmurs or secret scoffs, despise them; they will not last. Just say you wish to compel no one, but that you will feel pleased with those who conform to your wishes. From the very first, you may be sure, the greater number will come to the prayers, and in a few days all will do so. Try it, and leave the rest to God, who undoubtedly will second your pious endeavours.

Yes, my God, were it for no other reason than to impose on myself the obligation of regularly discharging so holy a duty, I will establish family prayers in my house. Moreover, I am bound to give good example to my children and servants, and bound likewise to make sure that they render Thee daily the homage which is due to Thee. I am a father and a master; and these titles which I hold from Thee give me a right to enforce obligations of which the chief incontestably is to see Thee honoured and served by my dependants. From Thee is my authority, and it is but just that I should employ it in seeing Thee duly worshipped. Forgive, O Lord! my past neglect in this respect. I am resolved to repair it. Perhaps I have been a cause of scandal to my household; henceforth I am resolved to give edification. I am answerable to Thee for the conduct of my children and servants, and it is important to my salvation that I should be able to give a good account of them. Bless the resolution I take in Thy presence and give me the grace to be faithful to it every day of my life. *Amen.*

CHAPTER X.

THE LORD'S PRAYER.

THE Lord's Prayer was the fruit of the request which the Apostles, inspired by the Holy Ghost, made to our Blessed Lord when they said to Him: " *Lord, teach us to pray!* "* It is a divine prayer, whether we consider its Author or the sentiments it expresses; a prayer that Jesus Christ has taught us all, in the person of the Apostles whom He desired should instruct all nations; a prayer that the Church places above all others, that forms an integral part of the sacrifice of our Altars, where it is never omitted; she begins all her offices with it, she teaches children to say it in their earliest years, explains it to them in all her Catechisms, and recommends the faithful to repeat it many times a day, especially in the morning and evening. This prayer, in fact, contains everything. Our Blessed Saviour, who knew our duties and our wants, has, in few words, comprised them in it. A Christian can say nothing to the praise of God, nor ask Him for anything that is not included in it. By its

---

* *Luke* xi. 2.

simplicity it is within the reach of everyone; by the sublimity of its thoughts, it surpasses the power of intellect of the highest genius, and, to understand it, we must have nothing less than supernatural light.   But it is more for the heart than for the head, and this from the very nature of the prayer ; and, although it may be necessary to understand it, it is far more important that it should be felt.   Our Lord's intention in teaching it, could not be that it should be confined to the recitation merely.   He wished it to be understood that we should adopt its sentiments, and that we make it our rule of life.   There is not a Christian who does not know it by heart : it is the chief and most frequently repeated of all our prayers.   But do we understand it ?   Have we thoroughly searched into its meaning ?   Have we ever asked our Lord that He Himself would open our mind to its meaning ?   Are there many Christians even among the most pious, who have the humility necessary to acknowledge that they do not understand it ; who are so enlightened by God as to know that they cannot understand it if they are not spiritually minded, and unless the same Holy Spirit who dictated it explains it to them ?

Yet this is not the essential point.   Is it not from habit and mechanically that we recite this prayer ?   Does our heart feel it ?   Is it the expression of our inmost thoughts ?   Can we say after each word, after each petition: "This is what I think, what I feel, what I desire?" If we have not habitually in our soul the feelings it expresses, let us not flatter ourselves that we are good Christians.

Finally, do we believe that this prayer is the most indispensable rule of life, as it is the most excellent? Do we believe it to be an epitome of the Gospel, an extract of all that is most perfect, in the moral teaching of Jesus Christ, and consequently that it must influence our thoughts, words, and actions? And in practice, do we judge, speak, and act, in conformity with it? Would our life bear comparison with it? This is what I would exhort every one to reflect upon seriously.

Why do we pray? That we may live well. What do we ask for when we pray? That we may do our duty. We are not now speaking of a prayer composed for our devotion and by men. Jesus Christ gave it to us, and in drawing it up did not consult our ideas, but His own; and when He said: "*Thus will you pray*," He says to us equivalently: "You must rule your life according to the spirit of this prayer. If you do not you will be condemned by your own lips. Every day you asked Me for this, and your conduct gave the lie to your requests; and you never thought that there was an essential connection between your prayer and your actions."

As it is a certain fact that we shall one day be judged by Jesus Christ on the prayer that bears His name, let us for awhile give our attention and application to understanding its meaning, and weighing the obligations it imposes on us.

With the help of God's grace I am going to undertake the explanation of this prayer, not forgetting I am working as much and more for myself as for others.

Our Father!

It is to my Father I address myself.

Never should I myself have dared, sinner as I am, to give this title to God, or consider myself His child. Jesus Christ inspires me with the boldness to do so. He begins by reminding me that grace has made me a child of God—this I am by adoption; I have been raised to this glorious privilege by the ineffable mystery of the union of the Word with His Sacred Humanity. As man, Jesus Christ is my brother; after His resurrection He calls His disciples by this name, and in them He included us all. In the Gospel He constantly says: " *My Father* and *your Father*," placing us, so to speak, in the same rank and degree of proximity with God as Himself, and authorising us, even obliging us, to share His nature and His reward.

Let us go back further and consider in their

origin and in their consequences, foundations of this divine paternity in our regard.

God is my Father by creation.

My entire being is from Him. The share which the authors of my birth had in the existence of my body may almost be counted for nothing; they were the occasion of it, simply the instruments acting under the laws instituted by God. It is He who created the matter, He who formed it in my mother's womb. It is He who placed in it the source of life and movement, who gave it nourishment and growth. How much more then is He my Father than those of whom I am born! And if I owe them respect, love and obedience, how much the more do I owe God, who has greater and unlimited rights on the work of His Hands!

It is little that He is the Creator and Architect of the inferior part of myself. My soul, that intellectual substance which by its nature is free, spiritual, and immortal, my soul made to the image of God is from Him, and solely from Him. My parents in no way contributed to its existence; at the very most they unknowingly determined the time of its creation. This soul then has absolutely no Father but God. To Him is it beholden for its being, its powers, its qualities. He made it what it is, because He so willed. This was an act of pure kindness, for He had no need of it, being perfectly happy and independent of it. Here then is assuredly a title to paternity very superior to that of my earthly parents.

There is still another very considerable difference. In whatever way I may hold my existence from my parents, they gave it to me by a passing act. It was not in their power to preserve it in me, and in spite of all their tender care and kindness it was liable to be taken from me at any moment. But the action by which God created me continues always; if it ceased for a single moment my body and soul would return to nothingness. So that not only is He my Father, but He continues to be such without interruption; until I breathe my last sigh it is He that preserves the life of my body; after death He preserves that of my soul; and when at the general resurrection He re-unites my body and soul, He will preserve both the one and the other for all eternity. Thus He was, is, and always will be my Father, as long as I shall exist; and my soul will never cease to exist, whether it be separate from, united to, or re-united to my body. My dependence on Him for existence being so great, and the benefit of His Paternity so lasting, what then should be my love for Him and my gratitude to Him!

Yet what God is to me in the order of nature, is little compared to what He is in the order of grace, where He shows Himself to be my Father in an infinitely more excellent manner. To have created me is certainly a great benefit; it is the beginning and foundation of all the rest. It is a benefit that could come only from a Being infinite in power, goodness, and liberality. But to have created me in His friendship and grace; to have adorned my soul at the very moment that it came fresh from His hands with supernatural gifts; to have destined it to possess and love, and eternally enjoy the same happiness as Himself. This is a new kind of benefit incomparably surpassing the first. Child of God by my birth, I am so in a far higher sense, and more intimate manner by what He destines for me. This draws me nearer to Him, unites me inseparably to Him, and morally makes of Him and of me but one being, having but one will and a joint possession of the same goods. I was by no means entitled to such a destiny; I might have been deprived of it without any right to complain. I should even have been ignorant of my capacity for it if God had not deigned to reveal it to me.

It is only after the death of their earthly fathers that children are called to the possession of their estate. They only enjoy it by title of succession and inheritance, and they only increase in riches by being deprived of what is most dear to them. Parents do not give their estate to their children, they only leave them what they can no longer

K

keep ; **and** if in their lifetime they part with **a** portion, they always retain the capital as long **as** they live.   It is not thus that our Heavenly Father acts, who, incapable of death, has nothing to leave after Him.   He is eager to give us **all** He has, and all He is ; and after the short trial of a temporal life, which would have been a happy one if sin had not entered, He had designed to admit us to the enjoyment of eternal life.   **To** attain this second life, we had not even to pass through death ; such was our original condition. Fatherly goodness of God, couldst Thou go beyond this ?   To be loved by me hast Thou not done more than I could have dared hope or desire ?   But there is a proof of Fatherly love more marvellous still.

Man, although laden with so many graces, **and** destined to so great happiness, proved a prevaricator from the very beginning.   The first man and the first woman rebelled against their Creator and their Father, and through the most foolish pride they disobeyed His command, in the hope that this transgression would make them equal to Him.   Behold them, with all their posterity fallen for ever from the privileges of their condition. They have deservedly incurred for ever the hatred of God and His chastisements.   Their only **re**source is in His mercy ; but He had foreseen the evil **and** prepared the remedy.   What **a remedy,**

O my God! Could it have been expected from any father but Thyself? Eternally productive in Himself, this Father had an only Son, equal to Himself. He sacrifices Him for the salvation of man; He sends Him on earth, clothes Him in our degraded and guilty nature, and by a counsel decreed from all eternity, in this nature He wills that He should be humbled, that He should suffer and die for us, and as a voluntary victim expiate the first sin and all those that have followed from it. Adopted in the person of this Son, *the firstborn of creatures*, all men are thus reinstated in the quality and rights of children of God. Heaven, which was closed through their fault, opens anew to them; more efficacious and abundant means are given them to reach it; and incapable of any merit as they are of themselves, they can hope and aspire to all through the merits of the Man-God, which have become theirs.

The Father has so loved these rebellious and ungrateful creatures as to deliver up and sacrifice for them the object of His eternal love. . . . Let us be silent; let us adore and love this best of Fathers, and consecrate ourselves to His glory.

I must carry still further this consideration of the fatherly love of God for us.

By whom was this sentence passed for our sakes on this beloved Son to be carried out ? No doubt by the devils, who, irrevocably condemned

to the tortures of hell, had become the irre-
concilable enemies of God ? Not at all. The
devils were but the instigators of the malice of
men,—man himself disowned, outraged, and put
to death the Son of God who had come to save
him. The blow fell whence it should have been
least expected, from a nation chosen by an
especial predilection ; from a nation of which God
had wished to be the Lawgiver and King ; from
a nation which He had made the sole depositary
of revelation, and to whom He had sent a long
line of Prophets to announce the coming of a
Redeemer of the world. Still the crime this
nation committed any other would have committed also. For on what grounds and for what
reason should we prefer ourselves to the Jews ?
We should have been deicides as they ; of this
there is no plainer proof than that by our sins
we crucify anew the Son of God.

It is then true that, with incomprehensible
goodness, God made the most execrable crime
of which mankind could be guilty, serve for our
salvation. He had foreseen this crime, and knew
that it would be renewed from century to century
by sinners on earth.

The blessings and favours of our Heavenly
Father that I have been laying before you, are
not so general that they may not be taken personally by each one of us. Every time we pronounce

these first words of the Lord's Prayer, "*Our Father*," they should come to our mind, at least confusedly, and penetrate our heart with feelings of the strongest affection, otherwise we only pronounce the words with the lips, and attach no idea to them.

There are, moreover, numberless blessings peculiar in ourselves. So many sins forgiven; so many graces bestowed; so many kindnesses and tender cares; so much patience with our procrastination; a guilty life so long spared, and which might have been cut off on the occasion of the first sin, without leaving any time for penance!

Let each one, as he says *Our Father*, call to mind all he owes to God. This thought alone is sufficient to fill us with wondering admiration, and make us fall into an ecstasy of love and gratitude at the mere recollection of such excessive charity. Yes, the simple word *Father!* is good enough for thought and love for a whole lifetime. No meditation can exhaust its deep meaning; no contemplation can attain the height of this idea; after nourishing ourselves with it here below, we shall find in it subject for praise and thanksgiving to all eternity.

Yet I have not said all: it remains for me to speak of what this Father is in Himself, of His nature and of His infinite perfections—another abyss where the mind loses itself and where the heart discovers purer and more powerful motives of love.

If "*the glory of children*"* are their fathers, what a glory is ours! What cause for triumphs and thankfulness is this thought: God Himself is my Father! With what a noble pride should it not fill me! What contempt, what hatred for all that could lead me to degenerate from so exalted an origin!

O my Father! how I feel raised above everything of this earth, when I think that Thou art God, that Thou dost exist by the very necessity of Thy nature, that Thou art infinitely perfect, the Sovereign Being, eternal, infinite, independent of all else; and that I belong to Thee, that I am Thy child, and that Thou dost glory in it! May I then not also glory in it? Can I not exclaim: Oh how happy am I to have such a Father! What majesty there is in Thee! What beauty, what wealth, what power, what knowledge, what holiness, what bliss! I rejoice that I understand nothing of the ineffable marvels of Thy attributes! If the sublimest of created intelligence was capable of fathoming Thee, Thou wouldst not be what Thou art, and Thou wouldst not dwell in inaccessible light. How wonderful too the union, and yet the distinction of the three adorable

* *Proverbs* xvii. 6

Persons who possess in Thee the same nature without injuring its unity! Who can understand the divine Paternity? Who can explain the eternal Sonship, or the procession of the Holy Ghost, who is the essential love of the Father and the Son alike, from one and from the other? This Unity, this Trinity which is the incommunicable property of Thy nature, is my glory, my joy, my happiness, because it is Thine. Thou art my Father, and the child is noble, with the nobility of His Father, rich with His riches, perfect with His perfection. This I am, by Thy will, as much as it is possible for me, and I ought to be so by my own choice, if I love Thee, and if I love myself in Thee as I ought.

O all-glorious, beauteous name! how is it I have pronounced Thee so often, without thinking of Thy meaning, without being overwhelmed with respect and tenderness, penetrated with confidence and gratitude! O my Saviour, and my Master! I have recourse to Thee; teach me to pronounce this word *Father* as I ought. May it never be on my lips without my mind being absorbed in so sweet and tender converse with Thee that I can no longer continue the prayer vocally. And what need is there of it? Is it not all contained in these first words? When I have said them with the lips of the heart, I have said all, and my Father has heard all.

Our Father.

Observe that Jesus Christ does not teach **you** to say *My Father.* He enjoins you to say *Our Father.* He does not wish you to say this prayer in your own name, but He has worded it **from** beginning to end in such a way that you must speak in the name of all Christians, who are your brethren, and of whom God is no less the Father than He is yours. As in the word *Father* is contained every motive for loving God, so in the words *Our Father* are reasons for loving **our** neighbour. For God being the Father of all men, He loves them all, and consequently wishes them to love one another. We should be wanting in love of God if we did not love our neighbour; because to love God is to pledge ourselves to love what He loves, and for His reasons and for the same end, love, as it is in God, being essentially the rule and model of ours. His fatherly love causes Him to do good to all men, to desire their eternal salvation, and to provide them with the means of attaining it according to the order of His divine Providence. We have the same duties in regard to one another, both for the temporal as the spiritual. It is little not to injure others; we must strive to do good to them, and do it when occasion offers as far as it lies in our power; we must desire their salvation and contribute towards it by our prayers, our conversation and example.

Let us dwell on this a little more at length and draw from the divine Paternity motives of love towards all men.

If God, taken simply as our Creator, is our Common Father; as creatures we are all brothers, and by reason of this natural brotherhood we ought to love one another. Even as regards the body we have the same origin; we form but one large family, that extends to all times and all places. You will tell me that if we go back to our first parents the degrees of consanguinity are very remote, and that love based on such a motive must be very weak, for even brothers and sisters do not always love each other. This is true, but in the designs of God this was the first tie to bind us together, however loosely fastened it may seem. But the distant relationship of our bodies is compensated for by the close union of our souls. They all came from the hand of God at the first moment of existence, and in this respect, the generations that subsist at one time fraternise, so to speak, and are in the first degree of relationship. Moreover, if our destination is the same; if we are called by our Father to the same heavenly inheritance; if we hope to be one day reunited in the same country, and enjoy everlastingly the same happiness; certainly this is an urgent powerful reason to love one another as citizens of the same City, co-heirs of the same inheritance which we shall share without any disputing, or rather that will belong to each one of us without division as travellers on the one road whose end is the same ; which once obtained, charity will make of us but one heart and one soul.   Why hate one another, why quarrel, why try to injure one another on the journey ?   Is this a disposition that can conduce to our love of one another when we are together in our Father's House ?

In order that peace and union should reign hereafter, is it not evident that charity must begin here below ?   Do we wish to leave this world with sentiments that would exclude us from that abode where the children of God are made perfect, and, as it were, blended into unity with Him, exempt from envy and jealousy, and happy not only in their own happiness, but in that of every one else ?   O heavenly country ! true home of our souls !   O centre of our mutual love ! O aim of our common hope ! Can Christians love you, long for you, strive to be worthy to find a place in you, and yet not be united on earth in the strictest bonds of charity ?   What after all is this home to which we are journeying ?   It is our heavenly Father Himself.   " The Creator's hand is the creature's home."   There He is all ; He does all ; He takes the place of everything for those who dwell with Him.   Is it conceivable that children hastening towards the same Father, eager to enjoy His caresses, who ought to draw nearer to one another the nearer they come to Him ; is it conceivable that they should be so disunited that they cannot bear one another, and even wish each other harm ? And why is this ? It is because of worthless temporal interests, that impede their career, and which if obtained, will deprive them for ever of the end to which they ought to aspire. Besides all that I have been saying, this heavenly Father has adopted us in the Person of His only Son, so that in His sight we form but one with His Son, and He extends the love He bears Him to us also. He has redeemed us by the death of this Son ; cleansed and purified us in His blood, nourished us with His body which is inseparably united to His divinity : He has showered numberless graces on us through the merits of this Son ; this same Son, having become our Brother, turns with an infinite love for us, all His desire upon us. The one great commandment of His law, sealed with His blood, is that we should love one another *as He has loved us*, and as His Father loves us in Him. Are not these fresh motives even more powerful than the preceding as an incentive to love each other with mutual charity ? Whether our neighbour be or be not lovable in himself is not the question. The natural qualities of the mind or heart cannot influence supernatural love, which has its source far higher. You asked what there is in this neighbour which deserved to be loved, when God has looked upon him? Pray, why do you yourself deserve to be loved? Answer me. . . . He whom God has found worthy of His love, do you consider unworthy of your love? Because you do not love him, is God not to love him? And yet if He loves him, how can you justify yourself in not loving him? Do you not see that you condemn yourself and shew reason why God should cast you off, on the same grounds that you reject your brother?

But he whom they wish me to love, does not love me; he speaks ill of me, he tries to injure me; and he has even cruelly offended me.

Because he is wanting in his duty, are you to fail in yours? Is it from the feelings and conduct of your neighbour that you are to seek reasons for loving or hating him? Nature may bid you do this, but not grace. And when brotherly love is in question, is it nature or grace that is to be followed? Where would you be if your heavenly Father had based His love of you on your dispositions and your conduct towards Him? Where were you when He adopted you? What have you been since you were adopted? Have your most grievous and repeated sins made Him disown you? And yet you would disown your brother! And you break all the bonds of charity, and think you have a right to do so, because he has offended you! By your own lips you will be condemned, and your heavenly Father will follow the same rule that you lay down for others.

Thus the two great commandments, to which are reduced the Law and the Prophets, are contained in the first two words of the Lord's Prayer; and the Christian should never say *Our Father!* without feeling the love of God and the love of his neighbour, with all the motives thereto, revive within himself.

Do these words produce this effect on us? I do not require that the explanation you have just read should come in detail before your mind each time you say *Our Father.* That cannot be, and it is not necessary. It is sufficient that you understand it once for all, and that your intention be to have the dispositions that these words require. Are you so disposed? Do you earnestly strive to be so? Do you habitually, by God's help, say them with this intention?

Has the following reflection, which is of the greatest importance, ever come to your mind? Am I fit, am I worthy to pronounce thése words *Our Father?* Do I love God and my neighbour sufficiently for that? If I am in a state of mortal sin, how can I dare call God my Father if I have neither sorrow for my sin nor wish to withdraw myself from it ? Can the Holy Ghost cry *Father* in my heart if by sin I have made Him leave me ? If I hate my brother; if I wish him harm ; if I rejoice secretly at his misfortune ; if I speak of his defects and vices, and perhaps make his good qualities and virtues the subject of my malicious remarks, and if it gives me pleasure to hear my neighbour spoken ill of, and if I incite others to do so ; how can I dare say to God *Our Father ?* Can I acknowledge Him to be the Father of this neighbour, whom I hate and pull to pieces ? Can He be mine when I indulge in sentiments so opposite to His ? Has not St. Paul declared that it is the Spirit of adoption, the Spirit of charity, which cries in us, and makes us exclaim *Father, Father ?* Does He dwell in me, pray in me, if I love not my brother ? I hope that your state of soul is not altogether a bad one. It is indeed towards God that you are in a state of tepidity and indifference, and towards your neighbour you entertain feelings of resentment or prejudice, indifference or hard-heartedness. Can you then say *Our Father!* as Jesus Christ wished you should say it ?

You see then that the steady resolve of always keeping ourselves in a fit state to pronounce these words, as a child of God should do, is sufficient of itself to sanctify us, because then we could never bear to entertain in our heart anything that would in the slightest way wound the love of God or the love of our neighbour.

Our Father, who art in heaven!

Our Father is in heaven, and we are on earth! Sad and painful separation for a heart that loves!

The heart would be inconsolable if it did not know that such is the will of God, and that this separation is but for a time, after which His children will be for ever reunited to Him in their Father's mansion. As heaven is the dwelling place of my Father, it must be my true Fatherland. Thus I am but a stranger on earth; it is no more for me than a place of transition. God keeps me here in a state of probation, that through my faith, the ardour of my desires, and my fidelity in obeying Him, I may merit to be called back to Him and placed near Him in heaven, whence my soul drew her origin, and to which she ought always to aspire to return. This soul, that is all spirit, has nothing in common with corporal nature; all transitory things are unworthy of her esteem and love; she has no need of them for herself; if she seeks after the enjoyment of them it is only on account of her union with the body, and of this mortal and perishable life, which is the consequence of this union.

What is this Heaven which is the dwelling place of God? Is it the azure canopy bespangled with stars that is above us and that Holy Scripture calls the *Firmament?* No; only to accommodate itself to our ideas does the Holy Bible speak of this Firmament and of the heaven as the palace and dwelling place of God. But there are many reasons why it is the natural image of the purely intellectual heaven where God resides. It is immensely far from earth; its vast circumference is of an inconceivable extent; with the exception of the luminous orbs that shine there, it seems to our senses a spacious void, where an invariable order regulates the movements of the celestial bodies, and all is harmony, silence and repose, at least as far as we can see it. While contemplating it, the imagination is lifted above the things of the earth, and disengaging, so to speak, our soul from the body, transports it to that abode of peace, and hence it serves to give us a rough idea of it adapted to our present method of conception into which something material must always enter.

Heaven, properly speaking, is God Himself—His immensity. There is not, and cannot be for Him any place but Himself; and when we say *Our Father, who art in heaven!* it is as if we said Our Father, who existest, and who dwellest in Thyself; whose substance, as simple as it is infinite, fills all, and in whom, as in a measureless and unlimited space, subsist all created beings. When the sceptic asks mockingly: What is heaven? Where is heaven?

If he does not know, he numbers himself with the ignorant and vulgar crowd ; if he cannot conceive of it, it is for want of intelligence ; if he pretends not to understand it, this is due to malice. I exist, even now, in the immensity of God, for where else could I exist ? But I am not there as I shall hope one day to be. I know God here below, but very imperfectly. I think of Him, but my daily wants, my business, the objects that surround me are continually distracting me. I love Him; but not with a purely disinterested love, but with one which my will constantly drawing me to outward things can transfer elsewhere. I possess Him; but rather through hope than in actual enjoyment; and this possession which faith gives me I may lose through my own fault. It will not be so in the next life. I can neither explain nor understand how my soul will then be in God's immensity. This I do know : that she will see God, and know Him with all the capability of her understanding, which will be proportioned to the height of glory that she will have merited. I know that she will always be occupied with the contemplation of God, and that no other thought, no need, no business, no object whatsoever will ever distract her. I know she will love Him with the whole strength of her will, with a love that will never be turned away from Him, nor divided, nor weakened. I know she will possess God by a most intimate and close union, and with the certainty that it will never be dissolved. Such are the chief differences between my present state which will pass away, and my future state which will never end.

As to the heaven where after the resurrection our glorified bodies will be, Holy Scripture teaches me that the heavens and the earth I now see, having been consumed by fire, God will of this matter form a *new heaven* and a *new earth* which will partake of the qualities of glorified bodies and bear a suitable resemblance to them. Oh! what reason then I have to sigh after heaven, my true country, the abode of my happiness, where my Father awaits me, where He invites me to come, where He shows me the place that He has prepared for me! Can I pronounce these words, *Our Father, who art in heaven,* without my soul being lifted up to Him with the most ardent longing, or without striving to disengage myself from all transitory things that hold me back from Him? Since my Father is in heaven, how can I be contented with the things of earth and seek far from Him an imaginary happiness? All I have to do is to bend to His will. It is He who has consigned me for a time to this dark prison, and He alone knows how long this time will last. He has placed me here that He may try my obedience and my love, because He intends that my eternal dwelling in His mansion shall be a reward to which I may become as it were entitled. It is a grace and favour from Him to which I have no right whatever; on my part it is to be a prize, a conquest, and all my care must be to esteem it as I ought, to long for it and to spare no pains to attain it, despising, avoiding, and hating everything that can turn my thoughts and affections away from it.

How much were I to be pitied, if, beset as I am with every kind of evil, surrounded by objects which do not satisfy and contain no real good for the needs of my soul; encompassed with false pleasures, false honours, false wealth, a burden to myself and unceasingly exposed to the injustice of men, I did not keep up my courage by the consoling prospect of those true goods, goods without admixture or alloy, stable and permanent goods that my heavenly Father offers me, and that I shall never find but in Him! Alas! I should exclaim at every moment, *Alas! how prolonged is my pilgrimage! My soul is a stranger here below!* What a journey lies before me! What a danger to encounter on the stormy sea of this world! When shall I descry even from a distance my haven and fatherland? When reach its shore? When be in peace secure?

O death! the thought of thee has hitherto frightened me, because I neither consulted the deepest wishes of my soul nor the teachings of religion. But henceforth, far from fearing thee, I await thee with a holy impatience. Thou art the end of my sad banishment, thou art the beginning, and the entrance upon my eternal happiness. It is thou who wilt open to me, and introduce me to my Father's dwelling. What after all is this life from which it is so difficult for me to tear myself away? A banishment, a long and wearisome captivity. Does not an outlaw who carries his misery from clime to clime receive with transports of joy the word of recall? Does a prisoner think he makes a sacrifice when his chains are broken and when he is taken from his dungeon and restored to light and freedom? Oh! will the hour soon come when I shall see my fatherland? where my Father will fold me in His embrace and I shall fully enjoy the sweet liberty of His children, and this for ever?

Christians! are these your sentiments? Has the frequent repetition of *Our Father* inspired you with them? What good can this prayer have done you if it has not made you long for heaven; if you still cling to this earth; if you cherish all that binds you to it; if each day you multiply and draw still tighter its bonds; if you place your happiness here; if you know of no other solid goods but those of earth; and if to them you sacrifice without regret the lasting blessings of eternity? With such dispositions never again say, *Our Father, who art in heaven!* You do not believe God to be your Father; nor His mansion, the dwelling-place of glory and immortality, to be your Fatherland. Humble yourself, be ashamed and confounded, sordid souls, unnatural and ungrateful children! You are unworthy of the happiness for which your heavenly Father has destined you, and you will compel Him to exclude you from it for ever, if you do not change your sentiments.

Hallowed be Thy name!

God has not, properly speaking, a name. Before anything was created, He existed alone; and since the creation, in one sense, He is no less alone, having none like to Himself. His unapproachable and uncommunicable nature distinguishes Him from all that is not Himself. Nevertheless, He has chosen to give Himself a name, in making Himself known to men, and He told Moses His name was Jehovah, *He who is.* This name, infinitely holy in itself, has no need to be made holy; indeed, it cannot be, as it is above all holiness; besides, who is there to make it holy?

What then do we wish for God when we say: *Hallowed be Thy name?* We wish that all men should know Him, adore Him, love Him, obey

Him, and give Him the honour which is His due. It is right, it is most natural that a child should be interested in his father's honour, that he should desire his exaltation and his glory; that he should exult in it, and that he should contribute to it by every means in his power. But if our desire be sincere, it is plain we must begin by glorifying it ourselves. The desire that others should glorify it is the consequence of our own determination to glorify it. If we do nothing for the glory of God, if this is not the chief of all our intentions, and the end of all our actions; if we scarcely think of it, and if our own interest lies at the bottom of our service of Him, it is a mockery to say " *Hallowed be Thy name!* " for being so cold and negligent ourselves about God's glory, we shall naturally be even more so as to that to which He has a right from others.

To what then does my desire and zeal for the sanctifying of the name of God oblige me?

It obliges me first of all to sanctify it in my own person, by consecrating to God my entire being, my thoughts, my affections, my actions, not only by never allowing myself to do anything to its dishonour, but by trying on every occasion to glorify it. If I act thus towards God, I may rest satisfied that it is not in vain that I say *Hallowed be Thy name*, for I feel in my heart what my mouth proclaims. I cannot thus study to glorify

God unless I aspire to a pure love of Him; and the purity of love consists in seeking first and above all the interests of the beloved object.

If I aspire to love God thus, it is impossible for me not to desire that He should be loved and glorified by all men, because they equally with myself owe Him homage. This desire will urge me to devote to this end all my strength, according to my state of life and my power. It will lead me to ask God how best I can promote His glory and zealously further His designs on me. It will lead me to think that the only object with which I am on earth, the only reason why talents, influence, authority, have been given me, is that I may see that God is honoured, and may consider as lost any other use I may make of my time, my liberty, and anything else I have at my disposal. I shall take care in the first place that He be glorified by all who are closely connected with me, by my wife, my children, my servants. If I hold a high rank, if I am in a place of importance in a town, or in the country, in the army, or in the State, I shall use all my power in seeing that the commandments of God and His Church are faithfully observed; that all respect is paid to religion, to its ministers and temples. I shall strongly resist all kinds of scandal, and I shall not let the promoters of it escape condign punishment. It is easy for each one to know what are his obligations in this respect; they extend to all things that he is bound by his position, or state of life to do or prevent.

If such ought to be the zeal of mere laymen for the glory of God, what must be that of bishops, priests, superiors of communities, preachers and confessors, whose ministry has for its primary object the sanctification of God's name? It is for this cause alone that they have been raised to the priesthood and especially consecrated to Him. They are responsible to Him for the glory which He intended they should obtain for Him, and He will expect of them a strict account.

Daily we say to God: *Hallowed be Thy name.* Which of us studies to sanctify this name to the full extent of his capability, as much as God wishes and expects of him? For such is the rule and measure of our duty. And which of us labours to make others sanctify it according to the same rule and measure? Every omission or negligence of this kind is blameworthy; and how far does this not extend! Let us judge of it by the words of St. Paul: "*Do all for the glory of God*"; in this he included eating and drinking, and he excluded nothing. This is not a counsel, but a precept that concerns every Christian. Would this holy name be profaned, outraged, blasphemed, as it is daily, if each one acquitted himself of his duty in this respect as he ought?

But how are we to fulfil our duty on this point? Rarely does anyone seek to be instructed thereon. Indeed, there are very few people, even those in the most holy states of life, who have seriously considered how far they are obliged to sanctify the name of God, and there are fewer still who in this follow exactly the light of their conscience. Is it then an empty formula that we recite? And do we think we have discharged our duty by pronouncing a few words?

Take notice, that in saying to God, *Hallowed be Thy name*, you necessarily understand it to be hallowed as much as it can and ought to be by all those who are bound to hallow it, beginning with yourself. Do you understand all that this petition or desire includes?

The name of the true God is not known to idolaters, who still exist in great numbers, at least in three quarters of the world. You pray that they may renounce their false divinities and adore God alone. You pray that He may enlighten those poor nations who still lie in the shadow of death, that He may send them zealous missionaries whose preaching He will bless, that He will remove all the obstacles that the devils and the world raise to oppose their conversion. If, by any means, you are able to forward this holy enterprise, can you, without remorse of conscience, omit to give your aid, or give it only scantily? And, if you were in Holy Orders, and God called you to this great work, dare you be deaf to this high vocation, and not say with the prophet Isaias: "*Lo! here I am, send me*"?*

The religion of Jesus Christ, the only Son of God, is held in horror by the followers of Mahomet. You pray that God may open their eyes to the imposture of this false prophet, and that He may destroy this sect, which is antagonistic to the very name of Christian, which for centuries has held sway in large countries where Christianity formerly flourished, and which desires to destroy it everywhere.

The Catholic Church, which is the centre of Christianity, is calumniated and persecuted by heretics and schismatics, who have separated themselves from her and weakened her power for the last three centuries, so that she cannot as she ought extend her sway over the whole universe. You ask that they may see their errors and unjust prejudices, renounce their obstinacy, and crown their mother's joy by re-entering into her bosom.

The spirit of revolt all over Europe has sought to overthrow the altars of God and has spread impiety and immorality wherever it has gained ground. You pray that the godless sect that

---

* Isaias vi. 8.

disowns the very existence of a first Being and of the natural law, may be converted or perish ; that the ecclesiastical and secular powers may take the proper measures to stifle in its germs their dangerous philosophy, and uproot it from all minds and hearts. In every place, all the different classes in the State need reform ; the clergy, above all, need more knowledge and more sanctity since they have to instruct and give good example to others. You pray that all may enter into themselves, and confessing themselves guilty, implore the Divine mercy ; and that in future, by their irreproachable conduct, they make reparation for the evils and scandals they have caused. In one word, you ask that society, families, and Christians, may be holy according to the degree of sanctity adapted to each state in life, and that God be glorified in all, as He wills to be and ought to be. The solemn prayers which the Church offers up to God on Good Friday are implied in these simple words : *"Hallowed be Thy name."* Have you ever reflected on this ? And do you begin to understand how wide is the object of this short prayer ?

Can you form any idea in particular of the perfection to which it calls you ? It requires that the first desire of your heart, the one to which all others refer, should be the glory of your heavenly Father ; and not simply His glory, but His greatest glory. It requires that you should seek it, that you should try to obtain it in everything, every day and every instant of the day. Not content with your personal efforts, it requires that you ardently wish that others do the same, and that they exceed you. It requires that zeal for the glory of God must inflame and consume you, that you should only breathe for His glory and never cease reproaching yourself that you glorify Him so little.

Have we got so far as this, you who read, and I who write?

Think of what Christ had in His mind when He dictated this petition and of the meaning He applied to it. Think how He Himself sanctified His Father's Name; and that it is chiefly in this that He wishes us to imitate Him. Think what God is, what He deserves, what He has done for you, what He promises you, what He expects from you. Can a Christian possibly do too much to glorify Him? It would be blasphemy to think so.

Once more, how do we fulfil the object of this petition? It is the first and most important. We are only so far worthy of the title of children of God, as we take an interest in the glory of our Father; and He will only glorify us as far as we have glorified Him. What reward could we expect from Him if we were to die at this moment?

Let us dwell a little on this ; the subject is worthy of our consideration.

Thy Kingdom come !

What kingdom of God do we wish may come ? It is not that kingdom which He exercises over nature as Creator and Preserver of all things ; the laws He has established over them always produce their effect. No creature can frustrate them nor withdraw themselves from their control ; and if by some miracle He derogates from them, He acts as absolute Master, and by a supremely independent will.

Nor is it the kingdom of His moral Providence, by which He infallibly leads all events to His own purpose, even those which seem to depend entirely on the liberty of creatures. The counsels of God are immutable ; what He has determined can never fail to come to pass. Man can not alter anything, because all is foreseen and consequently prearranged.

Still less is it the reign of justice or the punishment that God exercises and will for ever exercise over rebellious creatures, who have violated His commandments. This reign is, so to speak, a forced one ; it comes not within God's primary intention. It is we who by our obstinate disobedience, constrained Him to punish us, when He willed only to have rewarded us. We do not therefore wish God a reign that He does not seek for Himself and to which sin compels Him.

The kingdom over which we ask Him to reign is one infinitely dear to His Sacred Heart, and which consists in the voluntary surrender of our will to His orders, in the free homage that we pay Him, and to which we acknowledge He is most justly entitled, and which He exercises with equal love and fidelity. This supernatural reign, which is the source of the glory of God and of our happiness, is exempt from all constraint on His side. He commands, but it is optional for us to obey; He invites, solicits, urges us by His grace, but we are free to resist; He reproaches us, and excites in us lively feelings of remorse, but we are at liberty to take no notice of His reproaches, and we can harden ourselves against this remorse. In fine, we are left to our own counsel, and we may glorify God or we may offend Him. Any other kind of dominion over our free will would be contrary to His designs and would neither be a source of glory to Him nor of merit to ourselves. Such is the kingdom for which Jesus Christ teaches us to pray, and which should be the object of our most ardent longings. Nothing but love can excite in us these desires, of which the sincerity, vehemence and efficacy correspond to the degree of charity that is in us.

This kingdom of grace lasts only for our mortal life ; and it will be followed by an eternal kingdom, where God will crown our obedience and make it His glory to be our happiness. This second kingdom is the end and aim of the first ; and God will only reign over us for eternity as far as we shall have submitted to the empire of His grace in this life. It is our duty to desire these two kingdoms more for God's sake than our own, because we should have His glory more at heart than our own happiness.

But it is above all the kingdom of grace that we must ask for, the more so as it is the one of which God is most jealous, the one which really honours Him, and of which He will never lose sight in the next life, where He will say to each one of His servants : " Because by your free consent I reigned over you, come now and reign with Me, and receive the reward due to you for having, in spite of what it cost you, been faithful to Me till the end."

We must not deceive ourselves. The temporal kingdom of God necessarily requires sacrifices on our part, and even, to speak more correctly, one continual sacrifice. Everything within us and around us is opposed to His empire ; everything inclines us to shake off His yoke, and it is only by dint of struggling and combating that we can persevere in obedience till death. There would be much less glory for God, if we felt less difficulty in submitting ourselves ; and a crown such as we are promised certainly deserves the most arduous labour and painful efforts on our part. Besides, this labour and these efforts are the consequence of the corruption of our nature; and this corruption is the effect of sin, that God allowed but did not will. If Adam had persevered in a state of innocence ; if we ourselves were careful to keep in the state of sanctifying grace that we received at baptism, we should only feel sweetness and ease in the reign of God within us. We must then only attribute to ourselves all that is hard or trouble-some in it. Let us then resist our evil inclinations whence come all obstacles ; and let us bless God for the powerful helps that He gives us to triumph over them.

Every day we say *Thy kingdom come !* but do we pronounce these words from our heart ? And do we do all in our power to advance this kingdom ? Grace is the instrument with which God means to exercise His power. Are we sub-missive to His grace, and ever attentive to listen to it, following it when we know what it requires of us ? Does God reign over our senses ? and are we always careful to keep a strict guard over them ? Does He reign over our imagination ? or do we suffer it to run wild and carry us on to evil ? Does He rule over our passions ? and are we careful to repress the first movements that would draw us on to sin? Does He reign supreme over our intellect; and do we study to conform our ideas to His and judge of things even as He judges of them? Is our will subject to His? Or do we not sometimes, nay, very often, resist? Are we not impatient under the least contradiction, rebellious against the designs of Providence when they do not accommodate themselves to our own views or plans or inclinations?

Where is the soul over which God reigns supremely and without contradiction? or at least where is the soul that grieves over the opposition she places to the dominion of God, that humbles herself and begs without ceasing to be made more pliable and docile, and unites to prayer her strenuous efforts to become so? How rarely are such Christians to be found, not only in the turmoil of the world, where certainly the devil has more votaries than God; but even in the sanctuary of the cloister! Not that I mean to say that the opposition of truly pious people to God's Kingdom goes so far as open rebellion; I am far from having so false an opinion of them. There are still a great number of Christians who are resolved to die rather than violate seriously and deliberately any one commandment of God or His Church. But is the Kingdom of God limited to

M

this ? And can we flatter ourselves that we obey Him through love if we intend to go no further ? Does not God expect more from us ? And would Jesus Christ have limited the meaning of the prayer He teaches us, to not resisting His Father's orders under pain of incurring His anger ? That cannot be. An earthly father expects and has the right to expect much more from his children. God, who has infinitely superior claims, wishes to reign over us absolutely and supremely. It is this that Jesus Christ meant, and thus are we to understand His words. This complete and perfect reign includes everything, and does not leave us the uncontrolled disposal of any thought, word or action. God must by His grace rule, govern and hold completely under Him, in all time, in every place and under all circumstances. We must withdraw nothing from His dominion ; the smallest thing would rouse His jealousy.

"Then," you will say, "can I dispose of myself in nothing and in no way ? " No, not apart from God, for you renounce this when you say *Thy Kingdom come !* and if such is not your intention, you give to these words a meaning which God rejects. The Kingdom of God must necessarily partake of the infinity of His nature, and you must not compare it to the kingdom of men whose rights are always limited. God's rights have not and can not have limits; and if you put any, you debase His empire.

I cannot insist too much on this point because pride and self-love always tend to minimise our subjection.

Must not reason in virtue of your human nature preside over your conduct, so that you do nothing of which reason disapproves? And what is this reason that imposes such a law on man, if not the eternal reason? Must we not also as Christians, creatures destined to a supernatural end, be guided by grace in all the actions which we are bound to direct towards this end, and which consequently must be performed from a supernatural motive? This they never can be, unless God animates and directs them by a special movement of His power. Reason and grace are then the two means by which God exercises His dominion over us; and the co-operation of both the one and the other is necessary that you may be subject to Him as a man and as a Christian. To this there is no exception; by this you can measure the extent of God's dominion over you and your voluntary dependence on Him. Do not say, " I shall not be lost if I impair God's right in small things; and who would be saved if His Kingdom is to be extended to such a high degree of perfection? " I answer **you** plainly that **a Christian** who think**s** this does not enter into the spirit of the Lord's Prayer, and that he is far from thinking as he ought. Take notice that your salvation is only secondary in this prayer; and that the Kingdom of God, much more important in itself than in regard to you, takes the first place. The question is not how far you are to make God's Kingdom reign in you so as to secure your salvation. Who could determine this exactly? No one in the world; and even your own interest forbids you to enter on such a discussion, where you would run great risk of deceiving yourself.

Even if it were possible to settle this question, is it seemly of a child of God to dwell on it? Does he not lower himself by the meanness of his sentiments, when he limits the rights of such a Father in his own interest, only thinking of himself in the submission he renders Him? You would be ashamed of such dispositions towards an earthly father, and yet you do not blush to act on these principles towards your Father who is in heaven. Rather watch over the Kingdom of God in you and leave to Him the care of your eternal salvation. He has all power, and He wishes it more than you; and He will secure it the more He sees you occupied rather with His interests than your own. If you love Him and can extend His rights over you, will you for a moment hesitate? His fatherly rule is so sweet!

No father ever exercised it with so much for-bearance. If His claims are without limit, it is because He cannot exact less, without derogating from His dignity; besides, if the glory is for Him, all the benefit is for us. He can lose nothing; but we gain all. Instead of narrowing the empire of His grace over yourself, you should wish this Kingdom to extend over all men. Give subjects to God. Pray that He may reign in your home and wherever you have any authority! Pray that He may reign over the souls He has given to your keeping; that your discourse, your example, your good works, your preaching, your writings, all your undertakings may be directed to winning souls for Him! Let the whole universe be included in your intention when you say: *Thy Kingdom come.* Be extremely sensitive to all that touches the honour of religion, the propagation of the faith, the increasing of re-ligion. Even if you should have to spend your whole self in labour, to suffer the greatest hard-ships and trials, nay, to shed your blood for this noble cause, reckon yourself most happy; for happy indeed you would be. Such should be the desire of all Christians. The Lord's Prayer is intended to rouse them, to preserve them, and to augment their number day by day. May it from this moment awake these sentiments in your heart!

Thy will be done on earth as it is in heaven.

What perfection there is in this petition !

We desire that God should meet with no greater opposition in us to His will than He finds among the saints in heaven. It is impossible to wish or to ask for anything more perfect ; if we realised what it means, and if we put in practice what we ask, God would be as promptly, as punctually obeyed, and with the same affection and disinterestedness, by His children on earth, as He is by the saints and angels in heaven. One will alone prevails in heaven—*the will of God ;* it rules in everything and for ever and over all and without any hindrance ; every one unites in causing it to reign there. This is not all: everything concurs for its dominion, and no one can wish aught else but its perfect fulfil-ment. Why is not heaven in this the model for earth ? Why are we not in this the faithful copy of the Blessed ? It is the will of our heavenly Father that we should be so, and the intention of Jesus Christ, and He only taught us the Lord's Prayer for this end.

No desire is more natural for the children of God, no petition more just ; and he who has not this sentiment at heart does not honour God as he ought, and is not worthy to call God his Father. For God is no less the God of heaven than He is the God of earth, and He is no more the Father

of the Blessed than He is ours ; consequently He
has the same right to our obedience as He has to
theirs ; and His will, the source of all order, is
essentially the sole law of every intellectual
creature, whether he be still on the way or arrived
at the goal.   We are gifted with free will, that
our submission may be meritorious ; without this
it would be of no worth.   Free will is not given
to us to authorise us to do our own will.   Liberty
does not give us the right to dispose of ourselves
and withdraw from the dominion of God.   How
could we glorify Him, how c   orth
our eternal rewa   not our free will ?
It is for t ese two ends God created us, and by no
means to dispense us from giving Him His due.
The imperfection of our liberty here below consists
in the abuse we make of it, preferring our will to
God's will.   In heaven, as St. Augustine says, this
defect in our liberty will be taken away ; then we
shall no longer make a bad use of it.   It will be
entirely consecrated to will what God wills. " It
is not true," says this holy Doctor, "that the
Blessed will have no free will, because sin has no
longer any attraction for them ; on the contrary,
they will be all the more free, being freed from
taking any delight in sin, so as to feel no delight
but that of not sinning.   For," adds he, " free
will which was given to man at first when he was
created in a state of innocence was such that he

had the power either to sin or not to sin, whereas in his last state free will will be so much stronger that he will be incapable of sinning,"* drawing near in this to the liberty of God, whose perfection is absolute impossibility of sin. Thus our present liberty, which is a gift of God, does not prevent that His will should be our rule of life, as it is that of the Saints in heaven ; and that which makes their state of life infinitely preferable to ours is that they have not the unfortunate power of turning aside from this rule, a power which is the cause of all the disorder and danger of our present condition. We ask in the Lord's Prayer that this power may remain inactive, and that we may never make use of it, so as to withdraw ourselves ever so little from the divine will. Certainly we must struggle, and struggle hard, too, and without ceasing, to attain this. It is not our liberty, but our evil inclinations, with which liberty has nothing to do, that make this struggle necessary ; our evil inclinations are the consequence of our natural imperfection, and are considerably increased by sin. The reason why in heaven the divine will meets with no resistance is because there are no external objects to incite the creature to oppose it, or with power over the senses, the imagination, or the passions, of which some are no longer needed and others are satisfied

---

* *De Civit. Dei, lib.* xxii., *cap.* xxx.

with the possession of the Sovereign Good. No selfish mind or will or interest exists any longer. We see things and judge of them as God sees and judges. Thus, thinking as He does, we cannot be at variance with Him; we approve what He approves, and condemn what He condemns.

Moreover, the created will has in heaven neither desire, affection, nor settled purpose that may be called her own, or that springs from her own inclinations. She loves what God loves and because He loves it; she hates what He hates and because He hates it. As to loving and seeking one's self, that is entirely banished from Heaven. No other interest is known there but God's interest, and no other love but the love of God; indeed the saints are only attached to their own happiness in subordination to God's good pleasure, or rather they have so intense an enjoyment of their happiness that they are not attached to it as if it were their own property. Thus they have no reason for willing anything but what God wills, nor for willing it otherwise than as He wills; such is the perfection to which a Christian should aspire on earth; and for this reason the Gospel lays down the express law that we must detach ourselves from all created objects and deny ourselves. Why this detachment? Because exterior objects attract us and we are seduced by their deceitful charms, and we are tempted to give ourselves up

to them contrary to the will of God that commands
us to love God alone, and all else for His sake.

Why this self-renunciation ?   Because pride is
a principle of independence and self-love, and
of an exclusive love that makes us grasp at
everything to ourselves, and draw from selfish
interest the motives of our actions.   Thus we
are in direct and continual opposition to the will
of God, who cannot tolerate that a creature
should aspire to be independent, or concentrate
his affections on self.   So long as the Christian
does not strive with all his might to put himself
in the same dispositions as the Blessed in Heaven
he will not be able to do the will of God as it
is done in heaven ;   and yet it is what he is
enjoined to do each day, not only for his own
sake, but also for that of others.   God not only
meets with no obstacles to His will in heaven,
but at the slightest sign it is done with love
and joy, and the Blessed think it their glory and
happiness to do it ;   so that to conform to it they
are ready to sacrifice all else.

St. Francis of Sales says explicitly that " the
saints who are in heaven are in such union with
the will of God that if His good pleasure could be
any better performed in hell they would leave
Paradise to go there."*   He expresses himself
no less strongly in several places in his *Traité de*

---

* *Entretien,* ii., *de la Confiance.*

l'amour de Dieu. It is useless to object to this that such a supposition is an impossibility. We know that very well, but that is not the point. We are considering what is the inmost disposition of the saints in heaven, and necessarily it is such as we have described it. The reason of this is they never see anything, not only preferable, but even comparable to the will of God; and that, to their mind, His good pleasure is above all things without exception. If it were not so, their love would neither be pure nor well-ordered; they would love God otherwise than He loves Himself, and they would love themselves as much or more than God, and such a thought is repugnant to the state and condition of heaven.

This is the model Jesus Christ proposes for our imitation, and how could He, without derogating from His Father's rights, lay before us one less perfect? The Christian must aspire to accomplish God's will in all things, however hard it may at times seem, as soon as it is made known to him, without any delay or hesitation overcoming all his repugnance; fulfilling it with love, loving it for its own sake, holding it in the highest esteem, and giving to this motive so great a weight that it would suffice by itself to cause him to accomplish it with joy. He should glory in doing so, and know no other happiness than this, as in reality there is no other.

But does Jesus Christ mean that there should be no difference in the fulfilment of His will between the saints in heaven and men on earth ? He means there should be none so far as the intention and disposition of the will is concerned. And so it ought to be, God being, as I have said, as much to us as He is to the Blessed, and His good pleasure being no less our supreme law than theirs. Where then is the difference ? For there must be some, and a very great difference. It consists in this : our submission has obstacles to overcome, that of the Blessed has none ; we feel aversions and repugnances, they none ; we are always exposed to be wanting in respect, more or less, for God's will ; they have nothing of the kind to fear. But then, our obedience is a source of merit on account of the difficulties we have to encounter ; theirs is a reward. Because they have struggled and combated, they struggle no more ; they have overcome repugnances, they feel them no more ; they have been faithful unto death, and thus are assured they shall be so for ever. These differences, as we see, arise from their state, and not from their sentiments or dispositions and inclinations, which in us should be like theirs. We must feel a difficulty here below in doing God's will, in order that in Heaven we may not have the slightest trouble in submitting to it. The trouble we feel now, arising as it does from the perversity of our nature, should in no way influence the determination of our will ; on the contrary, this determination should be all the stronger and more generous.

Is it possible, you will ask me, that the will of God can be as perfectly accomplished on earth as it is in heaven? Is not this only an ideal wish, a perfection to which human nature cannot attain ?

If it were not possible, would Jesus Christ have made it one of the principal petitions of His prayer ? He knew our weakness better than we, and He knew also the strength of grace, and the power it has over a heart that is entirely devoted to it. Here comes in the text He applied to another subject: " *With men this is impossible, but with God all things are possible.*"* Man left to himself can do nothing, but supported by grace he *can do all things*, as St. Paul does not fear to say. It is possible through grace to have a sincere desire of doing the will of God as the saints do in heaven. It is possible when we have resisted, and for long hesitated and even murmured against the will of God, humbly to repent and make a firm purpose to sin no more, and at last to attain to a state of perfect conformity to the will of God. Human weakness, however great it may be, is capable of this perfection, and the

* *Matth.* xix. 26.

lives of the saints are a proof of it. This **did** not prevent them from being, even in their state of sanctity, subject to some slight faults. But these passing imperfections, that took them by surprise, did not alter their inmost dispositions, and they were no less dependent on God's good pleasure. Now, this is precisely what God requires of us, what Jesus Christ commands us to ask for, and to which the whole Christian life should be devoted. Let us examine ours by this rule.

Each day I say to God: *Thy will be done on earth as it is in heaven.* Do I seek this will in all that depends on me ? Do I submit to it in all those things over which I have no control ? Is this thought : *God wills it*, the chief motive of my actions ? Is it my support and comfort in all my sufferings ? Do I strive more and more to conform myself to this divine will by making the vain reasonings of my mind and the rebelliousness of my heart submit to it ? Do I place all perfection in not deviating from the order of Providence, forming no plans of my own, disposing of myself in nothing, and being content with all that happens to me ?

If, after making this examination, you can say that such are your dispositions, you repeat your Pater profitably, and you fulfil the intentions of our Lord who taught it. If you cannot have this moral assurance, you must not flatter yourself that you have the spirit of Christianity and of its divine Author.

At the same time, you are not expected to arrive all at once at the highest degree of perfection. Who does not know that the Christian life is one long, continual apprenticeship, and that there is always something more to be acquired, however advanced in holiness we may be?

Do not, then, be afraid of the perfection that is proposed to you, or make this a pretext for not undertaking it. What is required of you is a firm resolution to submit in all things to the will of God; a constant attention to the practice of this submission by doing violence to yourself when occasion offers; and sincere repentance when you have gone astray, with a prompt alacrity in returning to God on the first motion of grace. This is the rule of conduct you should follow, with a true zeal for God's glory. This is what you should wish for yourself and inspire into others, encouraging them on occasions of need by your words and your example, and helping them by your prayers.

If you find this also too high a degree of perfection, and think that for you God's will is limited to His express orders, the neglect of which is accompanied by heavy punishments, you lower your character of a child of God, you weaken in yourself the spirit of adoption, and you have not the slightest notion of the obedience you owe your heavenly Father.

Let us pause awhile, and dwell a little longer on these three first petitions, which contain a most important truth : let us see how these three petitions formed the basis of Jesus Christ's prayer during His whole mortal life.

What did He say to His Father in His prayer ? Nothing more than: *Hallowed be Thy name ! Thy kingdom come !   Thy will be done on earth as it is in heaven !*   Man-God as He was, He could make no holier prayer, nor have in His heart any purer desire; His life was the perfect fulfilment of these prayers.   Forgetting Himself, He was wholly occupied with the sanctification of His Father's name.   He only sought to establish His Father's kingdom ; His food was the will of His Father ; from His entrance into the world He offered Himself to do it ; on leaving it He sacrificed Himself to it.   Immediately before His passion He says to His Eternal Father : *I have glorified Thee on the earth ; I have finished the work Thou gavest Me to do.   I have manifested Thy name to the men Thou hast given Me out of the world.**

As Son of God by nature, speaking to His brothers by adoption ; as Master teaching His disciples ; as Leader of the elect, showing the way to heaven to the members of His mystical

---

* *John* xvii. 4, 6.

body, He neither could nor ought to have proposed any other prayer than that which He Himself addressed to God. What a glory for me that Jesus Christ deigned to associate me with His prayer! But what confusion for me if I have not the same sentiments as He; if I excuse myself by saying they are too perfect; if I am so unjust, so foolish, as to measure by the narrowness of my mind and the baseness of my heart, what is my duty as regards the sanctification of the name of God, the promotion of the kingdom of God and the fulfilling of the will of God! I have never hitherto understood all the beauty, the sublimity, the perfection of the Christian doctrine, and the extent of the duties it imposes. But now, thank God, I am well instructed and convinced of it. I see that I have not even begun to be a Christian; it is high time I should imbibe the spirit of Jesus Christ and imitate His conduct, since I say the same prayer with Him.

Give us this day our daily bread!

There is not a word in this petition that does not contain useful lessons. The first is that it is God, who like the father of a large family, feeds men who are His children. To deserve their maintenance, they must earn it by their labour and industry. This is the universal law established

N

since the first sin.   God said to Adam : " *In the sweat of thy face thou shalt eat bread.*"* The earth, which before the fall brought forth everything spontaneously, yields her fruits no longer, except to persevering cultivation.   This is the penance God imposed on guilty man ; it is only on this condition that He will give him bread.

Moreover He wishes that man should acknowledge he receives it from His bounty, and that he should ask for it daily; indeed, all labour would be fruitless and sterile if God did not bless it. It is not man that gives to the earth its inexhaustible fertility ; it is not he who gives to the seed the virtue of multiplying ; it is not he who makes it fructify through the fertilising rain and warmth of the sun, or who by degrees brings it to perfect maturity.

The labour of agriculture is certainly the chief but not the only work to which God has subjected man.   All labour, whether of the mind or of the body, necessary or useful to the well-being of society is comprised in the sentence pronounced against the first man ; and whoever does not work in one way or another, or gives himself up to a useless or pernicious life, does not deserve the bread he eats.   He has no right to ask for it, and if God gives it to him, it is but the consequence of that universal Providence of God, " *who maketh*

---

* *Genesis* iii. 19.

His sun to rise upon the good and bad, and raineth upon the just and the unjust."*

The petition for food and the other necessaries of life does not dispense us from labour ; it implies it, as it is thus we become entitled to it. Besides, God provides them to us in such a way that they need our care and industry to reap and preserve them, and prepare them for our use. Neither does our labour exempt us from the gratitude we owe God as the Author of all good.

By this petition are manifestly condemned all unjust means of acquiring property which would be unjust and hurtful to our neighbour. It could never be supposed that God gave what we unjustly acquire for ourselves. And how could anyone dare to say, *Give us this daily bread* if to obtain it he employs violent or fraudulent means, which God expressly forbids ? This is not asking Him for it ; it is snatching it away in spite of Him. Every man, then, whose conscience reproaches him with using unlawful means to amass temporal goods, is unworthy to repeat the Lord's Prayer, and if he repeats it he pronounces his own condemnation.

Give us.

It is not for yourself alone and your family that you ask bread, but for all Christians, since they

---

* *Matth.* v. 45.

are your brothers, without excluding other **men**. You ought to interest yourself in their welfare as your own, for you are all the children of the same Father. It is therefore a culpable avarice to wish to possess more than others ; it is a foolish pride to imagine it is düe to you ; it is a crying injustice to diminish or take a part of what belongs to them to increase your own share, and it is also a mean jealousy to envy them because God has given them more and you less. When you say *Give us*, you leave it to God, who is Master, to distribute as He pleases, and I do not suppose you imagine He should portion out according to your desire. Besides, if God has given you much, while your brother has not the necessaries of life, you are obliged by this petition to share with him and spend on him your abundance to relieve his misery. For God wishes to give to all; He commands you to ask *for all men* ; He does not understand this petition *give us* in a restricted sense to your personal needs. If then He gives you more than you need and leaves your brother in want, this is not because He forgets him ; He simply wishes to give to him through your hands, and to make both of you practise the virtues suited to your condition, and unite you together by compassion and liberality on the one side, and a spirit of gratitude on the other. Thus, when your brother asks you, in God's name, for his part of which you are possessed, and you refuse it to him, you are not only cruel and inhuman, but you retain that which does not belong to you—what you only possess as a deposit, placed in your hands for you to distribute to those in need.

Give us this day.

It is for the present day you ask, and not for to-morrow. *To-morrow*, when it comes, " *will be solicitous for itself*,"* says Jesus Christ. You are alive to-day, and you need bread for this day; and God, who has promised to see to your actual wants, is ready to provide for you. You do not know if you will be alive to-morrow. It is therefore a useless and wearisome anticipation of the future to think to-day of to-morrow's bread; God, who wishes you to rest day by day on His Providence, does not approve of your being eager to provide for the future. See how the child lets itself be cared for by its father and mother. The greater part of the time it does not even think of its wants. Food, clothing, and everything necessary is found for it without the asking; parental care supplies all its wants. If it should ask for anything, it is for some present need; it is not in its nature to hoard up, or provide for the future. To do so would show a distrust that would certainly wound the parents' affection. Have you forgotten

* *Matth.* vi. 34.

that Jesus Christ has more than once said **you**
were to be as little children, and that the kingdom
of heaven is for those who are like them ? Do
not then wrong God your Father by distrusting
Him ; do not trouble about the morrow ; He has
thought of it for you—foreseen everything and
arranged all. Avarice that has never enough, and
is always hoarding up not only for days and
months, but for years and ages, is here condemned, even though by so accumulating no
injury is done to anyone.

Detachment from all temporal things is here in
like manner enjoined. What greater detachment
can there be than that which limits to the present
time the possession of what one has, and thus make
it rather a simple use of things than a possession of
them ? To leave the future to Providence is also
here recommended; not that Jesus Christ forbids
a certain prudent provision ; He only wishes us
not to be over-anxious, and discourages the anxiety
whereby we try to ward off evils that may never
occur. Is He not right ? And does He not in
this do us a great service ? Is it not true that
the thought : *What shall I have to live on to-morrow ?*
poisons our life for to-day. The greater part of
mankind are more wretched on accouut of what
they apprehend for the future than what they
suffer in the present ? Yet up to this time, says
the workman, I have earned my daily bread ; but

who will provide for my old age? My business prospers, says the merchant; but will it always? And if it fails what will become of me? I have a large family, says another. At present I can maintain it, but when my children are grown up, they must be settled in life: where shall I find the means, and then what will be left for myself? My health, says a fourth, is my only resource for myself, my wife, and my children; but if I fall ill or become a cripple, how can I support them? And if I die while they are still young, what will be their fate? Foolish men! why give way to such useless thoughts that only torment and worry you? Eat in peace the bread God gives you to-day, and trust to His Fatherly kindness for to-morrow. These cares that undermine your health and are injurious to your soul, will not avert the accidents you dread, and which you see looming in the distant future. God alone can preserve you from evil; and what better means of securing His aid than trusting implicitly to Him?

Give us our bread.

Observe, it is for bread you ask; for the absolute necessities of life. So long as God gives you this He fulfils His promise, and you cannot complain. He is not obliged to give you anything more.

You will tell me that the absolutely necessary

should not be taken so literally ; it ought to be a rather wider sense. I agree with you ; but is it for you or for God to measure this extent ? If it depends on you, you will never think you have enough for your state ; and so long as there is some one in your line of life richer than yourself, you will always think you are poor because you have less than he. Do not then listen to your cupidity, your ambition, or the maxims of the world that places its happiness in unlimited wealth. If what you possess is honestly sufficient, desire no more ; do not regret what you may have lost if you can do without it ; and be convinced that in the eyes of the wise man, and with greater reason in the eyes of the Christian, competence is preferable to opulence for the peace of our present life and the security of our future happiness.

Our daily bread.

Your petition is repeated every day because each day your wants are renewed.

God, out of pure kindness to you, has willed that you should be in a continual state of dependence as to your body as well as to your soul. It is generally true that those who live by the work of their hands, or by some business, are more mindful of God's Providence, more careful to invoke Him, more attentive in thanking Him, and more full of confidence in Him than the rich, who see their future provided for, and consequently do not put their dependence on the daily benefits of God. It is but too common for them to forget Him, and they remember only the need they have of Him when they are in danger of sustaining some heavy loss. Then they return to God, and recommend to Him the success of their affairs. No doubt this is good; but how different this forced return to God and the habitual remembrance of the Christian, who receives from Him his daily bread!

How different it is with the rich who fear no want, and the poor who expect from heaven the alms without which they could not subsist, and to whom a piece of bread is a blessing of Providence!

But, rich or poor (and the Lord's Prayer is for all), let us enter into the mind of Jesus Christ when He made this petition, and let us be sure that those who are abundantly supplied with the goods of this world are no less bound to practise virtue than those whose share is small, or even are provided with nothing at all. Above all, let us remember that our spiritual should go before our corporal wants, and that to relieve the body, even in its most pressing necessities, we must never endanger our salvation. Many people think themselves excused for their sins if they commit them from urgent want. This is an

illusion; this is making for one's self a false conscience. The true Christian never compromises
his eternal interests; he never even harbours the
thought that the necessity of living authorises
him in offending God. Rather than be guilty he
would beg his bread, if he has no other resource;
and he will submit, if not with joy, at least with
resignation, to this humiliation. What a sub-
version of right order, if a Christian, who should
ask for nothing for himself till he has petitioned
for the sanctification of his Father's name, the
coming of His Kingdom, and the perfect accom-
plishment of His will, not only thinks first of his
temporal life before thinking of God's interests,
but to advance himself in life or save himself
from a passing misery, cares nothing for offending
this best of Fathers!

Forgive us our debts, as we also forgive our debtors.

The Gospel on more than one occasion speaks
of our sins as debts we contract to the justice of
God, and His pardon as the remission of the debt.
For this reason, to make the matter more clear and
intelligible, instead of the words of Christ the
following have been substituted, which have the
same meaning: *Forgive us our trespasses, as we
forgive them that trespass against us.* This con-
ditional petition is very noteworthy. Nothing
shows us more emphatically how dear to God's

heart is the forgiveness of injuries. He here makes the solemn promise to forgive us the sins we have committed against Him, if on our side we forgive our neighbour any injury he may have done us. And at the same time He declares that we must expect no pardon from Him if we are unforgiving to others. To put us as it were under the necessity of forgiving, He prescribes a form of prayer whereby we expressly promise to do so. *Forgive us*, we say to Him, *as we forgive;* that is evidently: *Forgive us if we forgive*, and *do not forgive us if we refuse to forgive.*

The revengeful Christian is here judged by his own lips; or else, as long as he keeps in his heart any desire of revenge, he must desist from saying the Lord's Prayer. A sad alternative indeed, however little be his faith! Jesus Christ foresaw how hard it would be to our pride and self-love to forgive injuries, and on how many pretexts we should seek to be dispensed from so doing; and to cut short all our reasonings, to silence us, and to overcome our pride and self-love, He prompts us by our highest interest: He makes the forgiveness of injuries the essential condition of the far more important pardon that we need, and each day beg of God to grant to us. Moreover, of all the petitions of which this prayer is composed, it is the only one which our Lord repeats and on which He insists elsewhere, adding these words: *For if you will forgive men their offences, your heavenly Father will forgive you also. But if you will not forgive them, your Father will not forgive you your offences.**

Which of us has not offended God? and does not need pardon for his sins? Which of us is not more or less uneasy about this pardon, and longs to have some certainty of it for the peace of his heart? Well, here it is formally given by Jesus Christ Himself: If your brother has offended you and you are sincerely desirous of forgiving him; if you entertain neither hatred nor desire of revenge; if, on the first step he takes or the slightest sign of repentance that he shows, you are heartily willing to be reconciled to him; if, on certain occasions, you even make the first advances; in short, if you are firmly resolved to pardon him in this way as often as he offends you, be at peace and full of confidence for the pardon of your own sins; you have every reason to believe it will be granted you, and you can say to God: *Lord! I have been very guilty in Thy sight; I do not deserve Thy grace, but I have freely forgiven my brother as Thou hast commanded me, so I hope, yes, I hope for everything from Thy goodness and mercy, and my hope rests on Thy promises, which are infallible.* Is there for the Christian, who knows of what happiness sin deprives him, and to

---

* *Matth.* vi. 14, 15.

what chastisement it exposes him, any consolation to be compared with this? On the other hand, what desolation, what despair, what a sad certainty of eternal reprobation if he obstinately refuses to forgive if to his dying day, and if he entertains feelings of revenge! His sentence is already passed, he has signed it beforehand. It is out of his power to say to God: *Forgive me.* He has had no mercy on his neighbour, and so he cannot expect anything but a judgment without mercy. He knows this: there is no truth more clear nor oftener expressed in the Gospel, and the *Our Father* that he has recited from childhood bears witness against him. Will he, as some people have done, suppress or alter this petition? Is he the Lord of all? Besides, what would he gain by this? Would Jesus Christ sanction this suppression or alteration? On the contrary: would it not be adding sin to sin? In what an awful state is that heart which is given over to hatred. It is an anticipated damnation. Nevertheless, this is not a rare case, and human pride is foolish enough to try and justify it. The revengeful man dares to say that God has imposed on him too severe conditions, and in his blind fury he charges God with injustice. What, you wretched man! you owe your Master ten thousand talents. He has pity on you; He forgives you your debt. And leaving Him, you lay hands on

your brother who owes you a hundred pence. **You**
throttle him, saying : Pay what thou owest **me** !
You turn a deaf ear to his prayers and supplications ; and do you not think it right that God
should deal with you even as you deal with your
fellow men ?   Man will not forgive his fellow
creature offences which are light, as being acts
done by an equal on an equal ; and yet he pre-
sumes that God will forgive him his sins that
offend His Infinite Majesty.   What an excess of
pride and injustice !   Is it not, on the contrary,
evident that God yields up His rights and that He
could not offer a more favourable condition ?   The
debts we contract against Him by our sins bear
absolutely no proportion with those debts men
contract with each other by injuries done.   God,
who is always disposed to remit all our debts on
the first petition we make for pardon, and who
wishes that charity and peace should dwell with us
(as He intends to unite us eternally in His paternal
bosom, in His home of charity and peace), could
not in order to reconcile us to Himself exact less
from us than that we should be perfectly reconciled to our neighbour.   And does Jesus Christ,
who, on the cross had our sins present to His mind,
and there shed His precious blood for us who crucified Him no less than for the Jews, ask too much
of us when He asks us to forgive each other, as He
forgave us ?   Nothing seems more just to our proud

minds than revenge; and on Christian principles nothing is more unjust. Even though we were not guilty in God's sight, the example of Jesus Christ would impose on us the obligation of forgiving injuries, and we should be worthy of punishment if we did not imitate Him in this respect.

Lead us not into temptation!

What do we here pray for? It cannot be that God should not Himself tempt us and put us in the immediate occasion of offending Him. God tries our virtue, but He does not tempt us; that is He neither invites nor impels us to evil. It is one thing to exercise virtue by trials and quite another to excite the evil passions of man. *God*, says St. James, *is not a tempter of evils, and He tempteth no man. But every man is tempted by his own concupiscence, being drawn away and allured.** It is not God who put concupiscence in man, it is the fruit of sin, and has its origin in the radical imperfection of our nature. This is what tempts us from within. From without, the devil, by God's permission, who has always our spiritual good in view, acts on our imagination, stirs our passions, tries to delude our mind with false reasons, and to prevail upon our will by attractive suggestions. His object is to drag us down to our own ruin, and to injure, as far as in him lies, the glory

---

* *James* i. 13, 14.

of God. This is why in Holy Scripture he is called the *tempter*. But God leads no one into temptation, except in the sense in which He is said to harden, *by withdrawing His grace*, as St. Augustine says, when man has made himself unworthy, *but not by infusing malice into his heart*.

Neither do we ask God not to allow us to be tempted. Adam, when in a state of innocence, was tempted; God allowed that he should be for His own wise reasons, although He foresaw the fall; and since sin has entered the world man is more subject to temptations than he was before. Besides, they try our fidelity, they are necessary to keep us in humility, and excite us to watchfulness and prayer. They can do us no harm without our will. Grace to resist temptation is never wanting except through our own fault. They cause us to make acts of virtue, and amass merit; and they are necessary to teach us not only not to fear them, but to struggle against them and overcome them. Even the Man-God allowed Himself to be tempted. What we ask for is that we may not give way to temptation; and that God will proportion it to our strength; that He will come to our assistance; that He will protect us by His grace against the snares and assaults of the devil; and that He will strengthen our will against the seductions of concupiscence. We say this prayer daily, because there is not a single day, nor even one moment, in which we are not, or may not be, exposed to sin. The home of sin is our own heart, and the roaring lion prowls without ceasing around us, seeking an occasion to surprise and devour us. Each age, each state has its temptations; the sanctity of our profession, seclusion from the world, even complete solitude does not protect us from it; and the most subtle and dangerous assaults threaten those most advanced in the way of perfection, if they are not on their guard. Thus, of all the petitions of the Lord's Prayer, in a certain sense, this one is the most necessary, for until our last breath we are on the brink of an abyss, always in danger of falling in, and death alone fixes us in the state of grace which in one moment we may forfeit.

This petition contains a double avowal, that of the corruption of our nature, a corruption greater than can be imagined, and that is only known by the precautions that are taken to be preserved from it, and the avowal of our own weakness, which is extreme and will never allow us to rely on our dispositions, our good habits, or firm resolutions. The slightest occasion, an indiscreet look, a passing thought, a desire that only seems just to ruffle the soul, suffice to overcome us, and cast us down for ever. Even after long struggling with a temptation, when we flatter ourselves we are free from it, yet if we pride ourselves at all on our long resistance, if we do not attribute it all to the grace of God, if we become less vigilant over ourselves, less exact and fervent in our prayers, the temptations will return, and assail us more violently and we shall fall. Thousands of sad examples testify to the truth of this assertion ; the experience of others ought indeed to make us wise.

Each time then that we recite the Lord's Prayer let us awaken within ourselves the consciousness of our misery; let us cast a look on the dangers that surround us, and on the enemies that beset us on all sides. Let us acknowledge the great and continual need we have of God's grace, humbly confessing that though with it we can do all things, yet of ourselves we can do no good at all. Let us never cease begging it of God ; and let us not make ourselves unworthy to receive it by our rashness and presumption. God owes it to us in virtue of His promises, and He never refuses it when through the dispensations of Providence we are exposed to temptation; when foreseeing the danger we fly to him with confidence, or when we are taken by surprise on unlooked-for occasions. As I said before, He is bound to give it, and never refuses His grace to those who are diffident of themselves, and who are intimately convinced of their own weakness, and so take all the means that Christian prudence suggests to keep out of the way of temptation. He never refuses it to those who are faithful in small things, in order that they may deserve to be faithful on great occasions.

The grace which God at these times bestows is not simply the ordinary grace, that suffices to justify His Providence and place it beyond reproach, though it does not prevent our falling; it is a special grace that supports us powerfully, and has always the effect for which it is ask for. He keeps this kind of grace in reserve to favour those souls who do all they can to merit it. I only speak of habitual graces, and not of certain special graces by which God sometimes draws to Himself the greatest sinners. The rash man who faces danger, without consulting the will of God; the presumptuous man who relies on his own strength, on acquired virtues, on past victories, or on the fleeting impulses of fervour; the cowardly and tepid, who neglect small faults that are called light because they do not kill the soul : persons such as these must not expect the assistance of divine grace in times of great temptation, or in certain difficult circumstances. They have of their own fault exposed themselves to danger; they have presumed on their virtue; they have weakened themselves by a long series of slight infidelities : they will have a lamentable fall from which they may never rise. Remember that when we pray not to be led into temptation, that prayer refers only to those occasions where God Himself has placed us: occasions for which an habitual fidelity has prepared us and disciplined us; at the most, to those occasions where, though our intention is good, imprudence, carelessness, surprise, an indiscreet zeal, and an ill-placed kindness, expose us to danger.

God, who sees the inmost heart, never abandons an upright soul that has no malice in it; and if He does allow it to fall, it is only that it may become more humble and more on its guard.

The world—I refer to that part of it which keeps to the outward show of Christianity—is full of snares; everything in it tends to corrupt the mind by its false maxims that tend to weaken the holy severity of the Gospel, and the heart by the allurements it offers to sensuality, lust, and ambition to love the world. To seek its esteem, fear its censures, its jesting and scoffing, is evidently to place one's self in danger of falling into the many temptations which are there met with each day; and it would be a decided illusion to expect that grace will preserve you from the dangers into which you wantonly throw yourself.

Still we must not be pusillanimous, nor diffident of help from above, whether in exterior temptations, that are the inevitable consequences of the state of life in which God has placed us, and the duties that zeal and charity impose on us; or in interior temptations that are to be met with in the practice of Christian perfection. We must expect to encounter mighty assaults from the devil if we choose to devote ourselves entirely to God. But we must not for one moment doubt of the divine protection, and must always rest assured that it will enable us to triumph over the spirit of darkness.

We must not imitate those who, struck with fear of being lost, fly from all occasions of working for the salvation of souls, under pretext of the danger of offending God, nor those who give up leading a spiritual life, frightened by the snares the devil lays in their path, and the trying temptations through which they have sometimes to pass. This would be insulting to the goodness and almighty power of our Heavenly Father; it would be to believe that the devil, who can only act by God's permission, and who limits his power, is mightier to harm us than God to protect us; it would be renouncing the work of glorifying God and labouring for our own and our neighbour's salvation. We must walk safely between the two precipices of presumption and pusillanimity, and then we shall never ask God in vain to "lead us not into temptation."

But deliver us from evil. Amen!

Nothing is so important for us as to know from
what evil Jesus Christ wishes that we should
ask to be delivered. For in all things, and here
most especially, His thoughts are the sole rule
and guide of ours; and it is of the greatest consequence that we should not deviate from them.
As the sovereign good of the rational creature is
the eternal possession of God, to which the soul
is destined, her sovereign evil is to be for ever
deprived of this possession. In this consists her
reprobation and damnation. The deliverance
from so great an evil is therefore the principal
object of our last petition. It is only through
faith that we can understand how great is the
evil of being deprived of the possession of God,
through our own fault; and yet, though our faith
be ever so lively, we can only understand this
loss but very imperfectly here below. Our weak
intellect is not in a fit state to bear a full understanding of it; it would make too deep an impression on our minds, and put a restraint upon
the liberty of our actions.

It is quite impossible for us to put ourselves
in the position in which a soul finds herself at the
moment of her separation from the body, when
she sees and feels that she has lost God for ever.
She then knows very clearly and distinctly what
God is in Himself; what He is in relation to her;

and the infinite and irreparable loss she has to suffer. All the objects that in this life occupied and engrossed her, are nothing now; she can no longer esteem or love them, because she clearly sees their nothingness. Besides, all is snatched from her by death; and if she can still think of them, it is only to reproach herself for her extreme folly in ever having cared for them. The desire for happiness acts on her now with all its strength and without cessation; and this desire, the intensity of which is inexpressible, will never be satisfied. She can think of nothing else, and no false pleasure can now delude her. Of this the soul is certain, and all hope is for ever taken from her. This pain is inconceivable, whether in itself or in its continuity and duration. No state of man on earth, however awful, however protracted, however hopeless it may be, can compare with this, because none of these states in any way correspond to the eternal loss of God.

This is the evil from which, above all, the Christian begs to be delivered, the evil that he must supremely dread, and which he must do all in his power to ward off. For it depends on himself. He has only to preserve himself from another evil which alone can lead him to the loss of God.

That other evil is sin, of which damnation is the just punishment. The one is the cause, the other the effect and inevitable consequence. The intention then of Jesus Christ is that the Christian should ardently ask to be delivered from sin, that he should not be allowed to fall, and if fallen, that God should give him a helping hand that he may quickly rise and not be overtaken by death in that deplorable state. On our first mortal sin God may cut the thread of our existence and cast us into hell; He may let us accumulate crime upon crime, and refuse with justice certain special graces, without which we can never regain charity. And, as we cannot be certain He will not do what He is able to do, this should keep us in continual fear of offending him mortally.

But, although that sin which kills the soul is the greatest of evils, every sin is likewise an evil, because it wounds the soul and makes her feeble, sick, and languid. A slight fault leads to greater ones; and if we do not endeavour to avoid the lesser, we are liable to commit the greater; the more so as it is not always easy to discern what is grievous from what is not.

It is not then enough, in order to correspond with the intentions of Jesus Christ and to place our salvation beyond doubt, to pray to be delivered only from mortal sin; every Christian should ask to be preserved from every deliberate sin.

Moreover, if he truly love God, he will make

this request rather that he may not offend so good a Father than from the fear of drawing down chastisement on himself. For sin is the evil, and indeed the sole evil in God's sight, not that it injures Him, but because it is supremely displeasing to Him, and it is the object of His hatred. Thus, as the Christian is bound to love God more than himself, it is right that he should have a greater horror of sin because it is an evil to God, than because it is likewise an evil to himself. This is the right meaning of the words, *Deliver us from evil.*

It is faith that utters them, and faith knows of no other evil than supernatural evil, that wounds the holiness of God, stains the purity of the soul, deprives her of sanctifying grace, or puts her in danger of losing it, and by this means exposes her to eternal misery. Are these our thoughts and our heartfelt sentiments as we say this prayer?

The Christian who knows he is in a state of mortal sin, and worthy of hell, does not sincerely ask God to deliver him from evil, when he does nothing to correspond with the grace of God which is offered him that he may free himself from it; when far from avoiding the occasions of sin, he seeks them, or at least gives way each time they offer themselves; when he hardly looks on sin as an evil and does not fear making himself familiar with his worst enemy. Is it not a mockery to ask to be delivered from an evil we do not fear, an evil we love and in which we take pleasure? Such, however, is the disposition of the greater number of Christians in the present day, who, nevertheless, repeat their Pater daily through the mere custom of childhood, without thinking of what they say and without applying it to the present state of their soul. God forbid that I should blame them for so laudable a habit; but the first and the least fruit they should derive from it, is that it should draw them nearer to God and make them forsake the ways of sin as soon as possible.

Those to whom slight faults seem trivial, because they only see in them the offence against God, and no danger to their salvation, are not only mistaken on this point, but they insult Him whom they call Father by troubling themselves very little about what offends Him, provided their soul runs no risk for eternity. Would not a child who only respected his father so far as not to get disinherited, have reason to blush for himself if he were capable of reflection and feeling? Could he do otherwise than condemn himself for only listening to selfish motives and slavish fear as regards the sacred duties that nature imposes on him? How much more guilty is the child of God who acts on similar principles?

The Gospel teaches us that the evils of this life are not real evils, and that, seen by the light of faith, they may be to us very great benefits by the holy use we make of them. Jesus Christ having chosen for Himself the heaviest of these evils, and those most repugnant to nature, His disciples must not make excuses for their natural aversion, nor judge them according to the dictates of flesh and blood, especially when they remember He took them upon Himself, in our stead, by way of a pledge and security. He made them serve to repair the injury done to the glory of God, and expiate our sins, and merit for us the graces necessary to preserve us from them and to blot them out. The perfect Christian will not therefore ask to be delivered from these evils, but will rather ask to suffer patiently that thereby he may glorify God, and sanctify himself by accepting them. As to imperfect Christians, of whom there is beyond comparison a far greater number, as they have not sufficient virtue to draw spiritual profit from temporal afflictions, but are only provoked by them to sin through their impatience, murmurings, rebellion, and despair, God does not take it ill that they should pray to be delivered from them. He accepts their faith and their prayers, and hears them for their greater good, even so far as at times to work miracles in their behalf. Still, He wishes that the principal motive we should have in asking relief should be that we may serve Him with greater liberty, more love, gratitude, and fidelity.   He wishes that, humble by the knowledge of our want of virtue whic prevents our profiting by them, we should pra to be freed from them, not to give relief to nature, but because through our own fault they are an obstacle to salvation.   In short, He wishes that no comparison be made between temporal ills and the one true evil, which is sin, and that we be determined to suffer to the last extremit rather than be freed at the expense of conscience We are not Christians if we do not think and ac in this manner with regard to the pains and afflictions of this life.

Let each one here reflect and judge himself.

To say this prayer well, to have in the hear the sentiments it contains and to put them into practice, is to be on the road of perfection.   Are we on this road ?   I do not ask if we have mad any progress on it, only if we have entered on it, or at least are we desirous to do so,—we who from our very childhood say the *Our Father* man times a day.   Let us examine our conscience on this subject and compare our dispositions with the articles I have expounded.   There is no examination more important, and, to induce us to do it well, let us remember we shall one day be judged by Him who taught us this prayer.

THE END.

WS - #0039 - 230922 - C0 - 229/152/12 - PB - 9780243106141 - Gloss Lamination